A Computer Called LEO

A Computer Called LEO

Lyons Teashops and the World's First Office Computer

GEORGINA FERRY

FOURTH ESTATE • *London*

First published in Great Britain in 2003 by
Fourth Estate
A Division of HarperCollins*Publishers*
77–85 Fulham Palace Road,
London w6 8jb
www.4thestate.com

10 9 8 7 6 5 4 3

A catalogue record for this book is available from the
British Library.

ISBN 1–84115–185–8

Typeset by Rowland Phototypesetting Ltd,
Bury St Edmunds, Suffolk

Printed in Great Britain by
Clays Ltd, St Ives plc

Contents

Preface

MEET THE £150,000 ROBOT THAT KNOWS ALL THE ANSWERS.

Puzzled? LEO the Brain Will Do Your Thinking For You.
Robots have begun taking over work which is too complicated or too laborious for human beings. In cold print this may seem fanciful. But now one is confronted by LEO, Britain's new electronic brain ... He is the only one of his kind on commercial work in the world.

Evening News, 16 February 1954

What is there in a name? Plenty if it is LEO, for it is a name coined at the dawn of computer technology, that has carried with it a long list of first achievements. For that reason alone it merits perpetuation. *Engineering*, 5 March 1965

To some, it was a supreme irrelevance, a quixotic venture into the unknown by a respectable family business that ought to have known better. To others, it was an enterprise of boldness and vision, whose ultimate failure resulted from the conservatism and short-sightedness of others, and whose story contains lessons that succeeding generations would do well to learn.

LEO was a computer. It burst into the British public consciousness through a snowstorm of popular articles in February 1954, although its genesis lay some years earlier. It was not the first computer in the world, by any of a number of possible definitions. As a piece of electronic engineering it was not fundamentally original. LEO and its creators deserve their place in history not because of what it was but because of what it did. For LEO was the first computer in the world to be harnessed to the task of managing a business. That business was J. Lyons & Co., renowned the length and breadth of the land for its fine tea and cakes, available in grocers' shops everywhere but savoured especially in the Lyons teashops, a chain of more than two hundred high street cafés.

LEO was designed and built by Lyons's own engineers, and its first programs were written by Lyons managers before the computer programmer existed as a job description. At the time, the few who knew anything about computers thought of them as tools for scientists and mathematicians. LEO was a novelty in that its circuits hummed not with non-linear equations but with the hours worked and rates of pay for the bakers who produced, among other things, 36 miles of Swiss roll per day. Rather than calculating missile trajectories (though it could do that, too), LEO grappled with the task of restocking each teashop every day with no more and no less than it needed to keep its customers supplied with bread rolls, boiled beef and ice cream. It even turned its attention to ensuring that Lyons continued to produce the perfect blends of tea on which so much of the company's reputation rested.

Fifty years later it is hard to imagine a time when the computerisation of such activities was remarkable or even revolutionary. Today we use computers not only for all forms of record-keeping and financial management but to go shopping, to teach children, to fly aeroplanes (and to write books). They have become an extension of more or less every human cognitive capacity, and invaded every area of human activity. Off-the-shelf software packages have removed the need to understand how computers work or to speak their language – instead it is we who are programmed to point and click. But to reach this point we had to start somewhere, and LEO was in at the beginning.

LEO's development brought about the convergence of two histories that until that point had been quite separate: the history of computers, and the history of office management and office machines. In this it anticipated by at least five years IBM, a giant of the office machines business in the first half of the twentieth century but a relative latecomer to commercial computers. LEO's creators were acutely conscious of their pioneering role, and were not slow to exploit the opportunities of their position. Soon after LEO's first public debut, with several applications running successfully on a single machine and interest building from outside the company, Lyons set up a subsidiary called Leo Computers Ltd, with the intention of manufacturing computers for sale to other businesses.

A background in catering is not normally seen as an obvious qualification for high-tech start-up companies, and Leo's later history showed that many potential customers and others found this hard to swallow. They made the mistake of judging Lyons by its best-known products: cake-making was seen as a light and fluffy enterprise, a far cry from the sparks and sinews of electronic engineering.

Nevertheless, the advantage gained simply by being first in the field meant that for a brief period in the late 1950s Leo Computers Ltd was one of the leading computer manufacturers and computing consultancies in Britain, if not the world. That shining moment of glory was achieved by a small group of individuals whose vision of what computers could achieve – and how to manage them so that they fulfilled their potential – showed a creative imagination unmatched in their time by those running any other business. Their story has now been all but forgotten, except by those who participated directly and the slightly wider circle of computer history buffs. As we move into a world in which it seems there is no business that is not e-business, it seems timely to look again at how it was that technology, commerce and management converged in a British catering firm to produce the world's first business computer.

Acknowledgements

This book would not have been possible without the enthusiastic support and assistance of members of the LEO team. I should particularly like to thank David Caminer for his careful reading of drafts and the unfailing courtesy with which he pointed out omissions or inaccuracies. Any that remain are of course entirely my responsibility. I am also very grateful for the hospitality of the Leo Computers Society who have welcomed me to their reunions.

In addition I should like to thank the following for allowing me to interview them: John Aris, Ethel Bridson, Mary Coombs, Joan Cox, John Gosden, the late Lord Halsbury, the late Derek Hemy, Peter Hermon, Ernest Kaye, Frank Land, Ralph Land, Murray Laver, Helen Jackson, Mike Jackson, Helen Pinkerton, Anthony Salmon, Raymond Shaw, David Wheeler and Maurice Wilkes. Steve Mitchell helped me to grasp some of the finer points of early computing. I am also grateful to the staff of the Modern Documents Centre at the University of Warwick, the National Archive for the History of Computing at the University of Manchester, the Museum of London and the London Metropolitan Archive for their assistance with finding documents and making copies of photographs. David Caminer and Ernest Kaye also lent photographs, for which I am most grateful. I thank Miss Iris Axon for granting permission for me to quote from the unpublished papers of John Simmons.

Finally, I should like to thank Christopher Potter at Fourth Estate for believing that this story merited wider circulation, and to Leo Hollis and Sarah White for bringing the project to fruition.

I

A Mission to Manage

The clatter of machinery was relentless. Light fell through the high windows on row after row of workers, bent to their identical tasks; but this was no factory. This was the Checking Department of J. Lyons & Co. at Cadby Hall in West London, part of the vast clerical infrastructure that underpinned the operation of Britain's largest food empire in its mid-1930s heyday. Seated at their desks in ruler-straight rows, the clerks tapped away at their Burroughs mechanical calculators, separated from one another by partitions erected to reduce distraction. The adding machines, solid constructions of steel and varnished wood, had up to a dozen columns of numbered keys to input the figures, and a crank on the side to sum the totals. Like a cash register, they printed out a record of the calculation on a roll of paper.

The three hundred clerks in the department, most of them girls not long out of school, had but a single job to do: to add up the totals on the waitresses' bills from the two hundred and fifty-odd high street teashops run by Lyons, and to check them against the cash takings banked by the shops. A squad of office boys kept them supplied with sets of bills, received from the teashops that morning in locked leather bags and sorted into numerical and alphabetical order by the office juniors. The senior clerks and managers, invariably male, stalked the aisles between the desks in their sombre suits, ensuring that every fashionably waved head was bent to its task; it would be their duty to follow up any discrepancies revealed as the streams of numbers gradually unrolled.

The Checking Department was one of three central offices at

Lyons supervised in those pre-war days by a young manager called John Simmons. Yet as Simmons surveyed the roomful of clerks and their clacking machines, all he saw was a waste of human intelligence. Punching a Burroughs calculator could be worse drudgery even than unskilled factory work for the girls who made up most of the workforce. At least on an assembly line, he mused, you could chat to the next worker or let your mind wander while you carried out a repetitive task. Mechanised clerical work demanded total attention, but granted no intellectual satisfaction in return. Simmons began to dream of the day when 'machines would be invented which would be capable of doing all this work automatically'. Such machines would free managers such as himself from marshalling their armies of clerks, and allow them 'to examine the figures, to digest them, and to learn from them what they had to tell us of better ways to conduct the company's business'.

Within little more than a decade he had made that dream a reality by persuading the board of Lyons that their company must become the first in the world to build its own electronic, digital computer. This was not, as computer historian Martin Campbell-Kelly has written, merely 'the whim of a highly-placed executive'. While occasionally unrealistic, perhaps even grandiose in his conceptions, Simmons was not a man subject to ill-considered whims. From his perspective, building a computer was not only logical and rational but essential to the good of Lyons and the efficiency of British business. Moreover, his idealism was not out of place in the Lyons corporate culture. Far from being surprising that the seed of business computing should take root and grow in Lyons before any other company in the world, in almost every respect it provided ideal conditions.

A Family Affair

To anyone who has lived in Britain for more than thirty years the name of Lyons is instantly recognisable. The fame of J. Lyons & Co. rested principally on its chain of high street cafés known as the Lyons teashops. Before the outbreak of the Second World War there were more than two hundred and fifty of them throughout the country, with the densest concentration in London. Oxford Street alone had six, while the closely packed streets of the City of London, the financial heart of the capital, revealed another teashop at almost every turning. They spread through the suburbs from Camberwell to Wembley; from Plymouth to Newcastle, provincial cities each had their own.

At its peak the Lyons empire also included grander restaurants and hotels in London and other big cities, including the legendary Lyons Corner Houses and the Trocadero; a food manufacturing and distribution business that not only supplied the teashops and restaurants but also delivered Red and Green Label Tea, Kup Kakes and Lyons Maid ice cream to grocers' shops the length and breadth of the country; and a catering service for large-scale events including Masonic dinners, Buckingham Palace garden parties, the Chelsea Flower Show and the Wimbledon tennis championships.

How did a firm founded on gratifying English tastes for tea and bland, comforting food become a high-tech pioneer? Behind the Lyons shopfronts with their pyramids of iced fancies lay a manufacturing and distribution empire launched with immense commercial vitality. The Lyons of the early twentieth century was a young, progressive company, eager to adopt new methods in both manufacturing and management. The company was founded just as a wave of social and technological change was beginning to transform the world of business; for the first fifty years of its existence, Lyons was riding the crest of that wave.

J. Lyons & Co. had its origins in a family tobacco business

established in London by Samuel Gluckstein, whose father Lehmann Meyer Gluckstein had brought him and his seven siblings from their native Prussia to settle in London in 1841. Jewish immigration to Britain from continental Europe in the mid-nineteenth century stemmed from the discriminatory practices of a number of trade and craft guilds, which effectively excluded Jewish citizens from many profitable areas of work. German and Dutch Jews settled predominantly in the narrow, crowded streets of Spitalfields in East London, and it was here that Samuel Gluckstein first lodged with his aunt Julia Joseph. Samuel and his younger brother Henry started a small tobacco business in Leman Street, Whitechapel, in 1864 with their cousin Lawrence Abrahams, employing skilled local people to make cigars and cigarettes by hand. But the partners fell out among themselves and the company had to be dissolved in 1870.

A few years after arriving in London Samuel married his cousin Hannah Joseph, and by the 1870s they had ten surviving children. In 1872 Samuel started a new, small-scale cigar-making business in Whitechapel Road, in partnership with his sons Isidore and Montague and another tobacco trader, Barnett Salmon, who had married Samuel's daughter Helena. Almost immediately their fifty-four-year-old father's unexpected death from diabetes left the young men with responsibility for the welfare of a large extended family.

Still shocked at their bereavement, the three remaining directors met to decide how to proceed. Mindful of the feud that had destroyed Samuel's first company, they shook hands on an extraordinary agreement. Adopting the motto *Union fait la force* (strength in union), they placed the assets of the new company, Salmon & Gluckstein, in a family fund in which each of the sons and sons-in-law of Samuel Gluckstein had an equal share. While individual family members undoubtedly had greater or lesser influence in the years to come, the philosophy of collective family ownership and collective family decision-making proved extraordinarily durable.

The family has held its property in common ever since, sharing all the proceeds of the business equally and owning houses and even cars communally rather than individually. Pushed to think of an exception, a surviving family member says that he supposes he might be allowed to keep his winnings if he had a lucky bet on the horses.

From small beginnings the company grew rapidly. To increase its profitability in the highly competitive cigar-making market, the directors opened a retail tobacconist's shop in Edgware Road shortly after the company's foundation. By 1894 there were thirty Salmon & Gluckstein shops throughout London. Three years later there were double this number, and by the end of the century it was the world's largest chain of tobacconists with 140 shops.

The shops sold Salmon & Gluckstein's own products – such as 'Raspberry Buds' and 'Snake Charmer' cigarettes – as well as cigars and cigarettes from other manufacturers. With Boots the Chemists, the stationers W. H. Smith and Barratt's Shoes, the company was among the first in Britain to recognise that selling through multiple outlets gave it the bargaining power to drive down wholesale prices, and hence to inspire consumer loyalty by passing on savings to enthusiastic customers. It sold its products at aggressively competitive prices, leading to frequent protests from small, independent tobacconists who could not command such large discounts from suppliers. Salmon & Gluckstein also made extensive use of advertising ('The more you smoke, the more you save!') and of gimmicks such as cigarette cards, now collectors' items, that could be saved up and exchanged for gifts. Their business methods occasionally verged on the unscrupulous: on one occasion they were successfully sued for continuing to label their cigarettes 'handmade' after they had introduced automatic cigarette-rolling machines. But while their competitiveness pro-voked indignation among their rivals, their success could only earn grudging admiration.

By the end of the nineteenth century the tobacco business in the

United Kingdom was under threat from the United States. 'Buck' Duke, the uncrowned king of the American tobacco industry, had used factory automation, national advertising, price-cutting and takeovers to give his American Tobacco Company a virtual monopoly on the booming cigarette market in the United States. In 1901 he bought a British company, Ogden, and seemed set to wipe out all British competition in the same way. In some respects the situation mirrored the predicament of the British computer manufacturers sixty years later, and the tobacco industry adopted the same solution. In December 1901, thirteen of the biggest British companies, led by W. D. & H. O. Wills, merged to form Imperial Tobacco Ltd. In 1902 American Tobacco and Imperial Tobacco agreed not to compete in each other's home territories, and formed a joint company, British American Tobacco, to market all their products overseas.

Salmon & Gluckstein had held on to their independence in 1901. But a year later they sold a controlling interest in their greatest asset, the Salmon & Gluckstein chain of retail tobacconists, to Imperial Tobacco. By that time, however, tobacco had ceased to be the main business interest of the Salmon and Gluckstein family.

Montague Gluckstein, though younger than his brother Isidore, was the driving force of the business and spent much of his time on the road promoting the company's products at trade fairs and exhibitions around the country. Entrepreneur that he was, he used the time to think about new business opportunities. He told his story to the author William H. Beable, whose *Romance of Great Businesses* was published in 1926: 'Any man moving about the country can, if he cares, pick up useful information upon the needs of the public, and he can then try to plan a way to meet them.' It was Montague's experience at exhibitions that 'first brought home to me the dreary and standstill methods' of the catering establishments he was forced to patronise.

The Great Exhibition of 1851, which took place in the Crystal Palace in Hyde Park, was the forerunner of a series of similar events mounted by major cities in the years that followed. They combined popular entertainment with the opportunity for businesses at home and overseas to promote their wares. They were the Millennium Domes of their day: the difference being only that they were hugely popular and successful. The Manchester Exhibition of 1887, for example, attracted five million visitors. But as he queued for an indifferent and expensive cup of tea, or ventured in search of a pie or a sausage in a neighbouring pub, the fastidious Montague Gluckstein reflected that as far as refreshments were concerned the exhibitions catered very poorly for their visitors, especially women and families. 'The ordinary man visiting a strange town and wanting a meal had a choice between a public-house, where he would get cold meat, pickles and beer, or a coffee-house, with its dirty little horse-box-like compartments, untidy shirt-sleeved waiters, grimy tablecloths, bad food and worse smells,' wrote Thomas Charles Bridges, describing Montague Gluckstein's experience in his 1928 book *Kings of Commerce*.

Surely, thought Gluckstein, there was money to be made from offering people at least a good cup of tea when they were away from home? When, in the mid-1880s, he proposed to his brother and brother-in-law that they diversify into catering, they were slow to agree. They were concerned about the risks involved in a new area of business, one which, as Montague Gluckstein himself put it, was seen as 'hardly the thing for people engaged in the aristocratic business of cigar manufacturing'. Eventually they concurred, as long as the catering venture was screened behind a different trading name.

The compromise was to find a partner to run the new venture who was almost family, but not quite. Joseph Lyons, an entrepreneur and salesman, was a distant relative of Rose Cohen, the wife of Isidore Gluckstein. Born in Southwark in 1847, Joseph Nathaniel Lyons had begun his working life as an optician's apprentice, but his quick imagination and gift for selling had led him into a colourful assortment of other occupations. He invented a device called a chromatic stereoscope – a combination of telescope, microscope, magnifying glass and binoculars – and sold it for 1s 6d (7½p). He wrote detective stories, music hall sketches and songs, and was a moderately successful watercolourist. He was married to Psyche Cohen, the daughter of an entertainer who later ran the Pavilion Theatre in Whitechapel; his marriage certificate gave his occupation as 'artist'.

Once the brothers had agreed that Lyons was their man, Montague Gluckstein went to meet him. At the time he was running a stall, probably selling his own artistic or technological creations, at the 1886 exhibition in Liverpool. 'I went there for a night, that stall was closed down, and the terms of our arrangement I put on an ordinary sheet of notepaper,' recalled Gluckstein. The deal they struck was that they would go into the catering business together as long as Joe Lyons could win the catering contract for a large exhibition taking place in Newcastle in 1887 to mark the Golden Jubilee of Queen Victoria.

Joe Lyons had no previous catering experience, and none of managing a business larger than a market stall. But he was cheerful, ebullient and persuasive, and he had the resources of a highly respected firm behind him. He won the contract, and he and his partners discovered, just as Gluckstein had supposed, that there was a vast, untapped market for the combination of style and good value that they felt they could offer. There was nothing tentative about the first venture into catering by J. Lyons & Co., the name adopted for the new company in 1887. Customers in the tea pavilion at the Newcastle exhibition were entertained by a Hungarian string band, they could choose from a varied menu and enjoy attentive service, and of course, they could wash their meals down with a pot of excellent tea for threepence (1¼p). 'Out of that humble but very important trio, tea, bread and butter of the best kind sold at a reasonable price,' reflected Gluckstein

The managers of an early Lyons exhibition catering venture
(possibly Glasgow 1888). Montague Gluckstein (in top hat) is seated
centre, Joseph Lyons (in bowler) to his right.

later, 'the foundation was laid of what was afterwards to be the
largest catering business in the world.'

Catering on a huge scale for exhibitions and similar temporary
events was to remain an important part of the company's activities
for the rest of its existence, but the Lyons directors did not stop
there. In 1891 Joseph Lyons raised the capital to mount a spectacular entertainment called 'Venice in London', complete with Italian
gondolas on water-filled canals, at the Olympia exhibition hall
in West London. The show ran for more than a year, and others
followed. At the same time J. Lyons & Co. won the contract to
provide all the catering at Olympia, a contract they held until 1978.

The association with Olympia was a factor in uprooting the family firm from its East London origins. First, Montague Gluckstein moved from his flat above a tobacconist's to a house in Kensington, next to Olympia. Then in 1894, the year J. Lyons & Co. was formally registered as a limited company, it moved its headquarters from Whitechapel to Cadby Hall, a former piano showroom and factory in Hammersmith Road, near to Olympia. Following the earlier model of the tobacco business, the company began to manufacture the products needed to supply its catering enterprises, beginning with bread and rolls from the Cadby Hall bakery. Within twenty-five years the site held a complex of red-brick factory buildings, erected fortress-like around a central yard; thousands of workers were employed on the site.

A retail chain to match demand to supply seemed an obvious next step. In the last years of the nineteenth century, ever-increasing numbers of clerical workers were commuting into central London from the suburbs to work, and they needed somewhere to buy their lunch. There were pubs, sausage and pie shops and coffee houses, and the chain of ABC restaurants run by the Aerated Bread Company. But these places, often known as 'slap-bangs' for the style of service they offered, had a somewhat sleazy reputation, and none was designed to appeal to the increasingly female workforce. The Lyons directors saw a gap in the market, and resolved to open a chain of establishments offering 'good temperance fare at economic prices in attractive surroundings and with polite and dignified service'.

With the opening of the first Lyons teashop at 213 Piccadilly in 1894, Joseph Lyons and his partners set standards of service to customers and sumptuousness of surroundings that astonished and delighted their clientele. Between the drab shopfronts of late Victorian London, the name of J. Lyons & Co. shone out in hand-carved art nouveau lettering, ornamented with floral swags and finished in real gold leaf against a white background. Inside there were gas chandeliers, red damask wallcoverings, elegant chairs

The Cannon Street branch was one of more than 250 teashops
open by the inter-war years.

and marble-topped tables, silver-plated teapots and fine china.
Highly trained waitresses, originally known by the name 'Gladys'
but later christened 'Nippies' (a shrewd PR move) for their speedy
efficiency, eagerly waited to take the orders in made-to-measure
uniforms with starched white aprons. The tea, of course, was
delicious, and only twopence (1p) a cup. It was an instant success,
with queues of customers patiently waiting outside on benches
thoughtfully provided by the management. Within a year the
capacity of the teashop had to be increased to cater for 400 rather
than 200 customers at a time.

The model was repeated over and over again. Two more

teashops, in Queen Victoria Street and Chancery Lane, opened in 1894, another dozen the following year; there were 37 by the end of the century and 200 by 1925 on prime sites in London alone. The provincial expansion began in 1909, when Lyons bought the Ceylon Café chain; within a few years cafés in Bradford, Manchester, Sheffield, Leeds and Liverpool had been converted into Lyons teashops.

The identical white-and-gold fascias became as much a part of London life as double-decker buses or underground trains. At Montague Gluckstein's insistence, the prices were the same whether a teashop was located among the department stores of the West End or the tailors' shops of the East End – another innovation for the time. Whether or not they drove the dramatic social changes that followed the First World War, they certainly reflected them. Writing in the *Daily Mail* in October 1921, and quoted by Peter Bird in his history of the company, Lady Angela Forbes observed: 'For the business girl, not only in the city but in every part of London, the nearest teashop is not far away . . . They share a table with men as naturally as they take a seat – or a strap – in tram and tube . . . From every point of view, and most emphatically from a woman's, London has changed for the better during the past 25 years, in that metamorphosis the teashops have played a meritorious part.'

Working on an even grander scale, the company simultaneously launched a number of larger and more up-market establishments, notably the Trocadero at Piccadilly Circus (1896), a palatial restaurant in the heart of London's theatre district, and the Lyons Corner Houses. The first Corner House opened in Coventry Street in London's West End in 1909, and was capable of serving 5,000 people at a time. There were restaurants catering to different tastes and budgets on the four upper floors, each with its own live band. (By the mid-1920s, Lyons had a budget of £150,000 a year for music alone – over £5 million in today's terms.) There was a food hall on the ground floor, selling tea, coffee and high-quality cakes

The 'Nippy' name and uniform was adopted for the teashop
waitresses in 1925.

and biscuits. You could even get your hair done, book theatre
tickets or avail yourself of that novel instrument, the telephone.
Two more Corner Houses had opened in London by the

mid-1930s, in Oxford Street and the Strand, as well as Maison Lyons at Marble Arch. They quickly achieved landmark status. 'In these places,' noted Montague Gluckstein with satisfaction, 'people made the astonishing discovery that beauty and luxury in eating were not the prerogative solely of the very rich, and the man of modest income and his wife could realise something of the spirit of refinement and thoughtful service which actuates the very best and most exclusive restaurants of this and other European countries.'

By the end of the 1930s Lyons had a total workforce of well over 30,000, making it one of the largest businesses in the country. Although its teashops and restaurants were the most visible part of the operation, food manufacturing occupied around two-thirds of its staff. As the number of outlets to be supplied grew, so did the Cadby Hall site and the range of products that Lyons made. After bread came tea, cakes, ice cream, confectionery and eventually ready frozen meals. The food production areas were highly mechanised: the Lyons continuous Swiss roll plant, which took in raw ingredients at one end and delivered filled, rolled, wrapped and packaged cakes at the other, was only one of a number of specialist bakeries working day and night. In addition to its own restaurants and teashops, the company supplied almost every grocer's in the land with Red and Green Label Tea packed by the quarter pound, foil-wrapped Kup Kakes and Lyons Maid ice cream. In London it also delivered to private customers, its blue, white and gold liveried vans even drawing up at Buckingham Palace.

In its unrelenting quest for quality, the company gradually brought many of the services it needed to run the business under its own control. The strong tradition of family ownership translated into a philosophy of self-reliance that pervaded every aspect of the company's operations. It developed its own printing and packaging, laundry and dressmaking, and transport and vehicle maintenance operations, and bought a tea plantation in Nyasaland (now Malawi). The attention to detail that had gone into the design of the teashops remained a feature of all these activities. The new uniforms for the Nippies, designed in 1925, which were still made to measure for each waitress, followed fashion by featuring a shorter skirt, and were trimmed with no fewer than 30 pairs of pearl buttons. The tea leaves that ended up in a packet of Lyons Red Label were carefully blended from stocks either bought at auction in Mincing Lane, the centre of London's tea trade, or imported direct from producers. Soft drinks for the restaurants were precisely graded, those for the Corner Houses containing little preservative and having a three-day shelf-life, while those for the teashops contained more preservative and could be kept for six weeks.

Despite its size, Lyons remained very much a family business. After Joe Lyons's death in 1917 Montague Gluckstein succeeded him as chairman, and thereafter the board consisted almost exclusively of Salmons and Glucksteins, fathers and sons, uncles and nephews. They tended to have large families, and there were many marriages between cousins so that the network of blood relationships was very close. The exception was the company secretary, George William Booth, who joined the company in 1891 and caused consternation in the early 1950s when he suggested he might retire – at the age of over eighty. 'He wasn't family,' says Anthony Salmon, former Lyons board member and grandson of Montague Gluckstein, 'but the family would never move without consulting him. He acted as a public conscience.'

It was Booth who recognised that concern for quality and value, and a fine sense of what the customer wanted, were not always enough to ensure profitability. The problem Lyons faced was simple to express, much harder to solve. A typical teashop customer bought no more than a bun and a cup of tea, costing a few pence. The profit to the company on that transaction might be as little as a farthing (barely a tenth of a penny in today's decimal currency, and even allowing for inflation worth only about 4p). Although the scale of the operation – 150 million meals sold per year – meant that overall turnover was high, the modest profit margin on each purchase could easily be wiped out if the clerical

Teashop interior, painted by Bernard Dumbleton in 1937.

work involved in recording and analysing all those transactions was inefficient. And since almost everything Lyons sold had a limited shelf-life, it was essential to have an ordering and distribution system that accurately matched supply to demand.

The same applied to the retail business: Lyons supplied goods such as tea and cakes directly to small shops, with no wholesaler involved, dealing with 30,000–40,000 orders worth a few pounds each in a week. Meanwhile, the efforts of the armies of clerks culminated in little more than simple profit and loss accounts – the concept of management accounting was then still in its infancy. That the business remained comfortably in profit during the 1920s

and 1930s owed more to Montague Gluckstein's instinct for what would sell than to any detailed analysis of the company's performance.

Booth saw that success in the long term would depend on a more systematic approach. In adopting this view he showed himself to be in tune with the most advanced ideas on scientific management that were then beginning to circulate on both sides of the Atlantic.

'One Best Way'

The term 'scientific management' originated with Frederick Winslow Taylor (1856–1915), a former Pennsylvanian steelworker turned engineering consultant. Taylor believed that losses to industry through inefficiency could be remedied through the application of systematic management, and that 'the best management is a true science, relying upon clearly defined laws, rules and principles'. He proposed that rather than leaving it up to skilled workers to plan and execute jobs in manufacturing, managers should analyse every task to reduce it to the minimum number of essential movements – the 'one best way', as he termed it, of completing the task. They should then allocate tasks to specialised workers and give them appropriate incentives to perform them at a rate that maximised their efficiency.

Taylor was widely attacked by those who saw his methods as inhumane, and he died a disappointed man. But during the First World War, when labour was short and productivity at a premium, a new generation of disciples picked up and developed his ideas. Factories were invaded by eager young men with clipboards and stopwatches, carrying out the 'time and motion' studies that were an essential feature of Taylorism.

In the years following the war, the watchword of efficiency began to be heard in offices as well as factories. The business office as we know it today was itself a creation of the late nineteenth century. When most businesses were still small, family-run affairs, all they needed was a few clerks in the 'counting house' to keep the books and write letters. The level of education required for a clerk was not high by today's standards – basic arithmetic and elegant handwriting were the main requirements – but as long as much of the population was illiterate, clerical work was a relatively high-status occupation. By the end of the nineteenth century, industrialisation had massively increased the size of manufacturing businesses, and vast new enterprises such as the railway companies had been created. There was an urgent need for staff to look after accounts, sales, marketing, personnel and all the other 'non-productive' functions of these businesses – functions that today seem to dominate the world of work, but which a century ago came a distant second to the business of making things. At the same time service industries such as banks and insurance companies grew to meet the needs of the large manufacturers, and public administration was also an expanding field. By the early years of the twentieth century governments were increasingly requiring companies to produce public accounts, and eventually to undergo external audits; the leather-bound ledgers of the past were no longer sufficient, and whole offices were dedicated to compiling accounts to satisfy shareholders and tax inspectors.

At the same time, the introduction of compulsory elementary education provided a ready pool of young people, both men and women, looking for an alternative to the skilled or unskilled manual work that had been the only choice for their parents. The numbers speak for themselves: between 1851 and 1901 the number of clerks in the labour force in the United Kingdom rose from around 70,000 to over 2 million. The proportion of these who were female rose from 0.1 per cent to 13.4 per cent in the same period; by 1981 it had reached 74.4 per cent.

The social changes went hand in hand with technological change, led all along by the United States. In that fast-growing country labour was scarce, and there was a great enthusiasm for machines that could increase productivity. The typewriter, patented in America in 1868, was taken up and promoted by Remington, the gunsmiths, who had found demand for their products falling after the end of the Civil War. In 1878 they brought out the Remington 2 typewriter, a design classic that remained in use for decades. Sales leapt from 146 in 1879 to 65,000 in 1890. The women who were entering the clerical labour force in increasing numbers proved to be particularly adept at using the new machine and so established their position in the hitherto male world of business, albeit at a low-paid level. Together with various forms of copying machine, the typewriter made it quicker and easier to communicate and to keep records of communications. Meanwhile, devices that we would hardly think of as 'inventions' today, such as index cards and vertical filing cabinets, revolutionised record-keeping. Adding and calculating machines, one popular version of which was patented by William Seward Burroughs in 1883, relieved clerks of the necessity to be accurate calculators themselves.

The office equipment industry boomed, led by a sales force that persuaded managers that simply by buying their machines they were buying greater efficiency. A dreadful poem published in *The Clerk* in 1937 epitomised this view:

> Early to bed and early to rise
> Is really very little good
> Unless you mechanise.

But others cautioned against buying expensive machines without first analysing the functions of the office as a whole. Chief among these, and the author of several textbooks on office management, was William Henry Leffingwell, a former clerk in a Chicago photographic company, who had risen to become a 'consulting management engineer' – one of the first forerunners of the management consultants of today. He wrote: 'The ingenuity of inventors and the persistence of machinery salesmen have brought about a condition in which the present-day office manager is not asking himself whether or not his office needs a machine of some kind, but what machine he shall choose from among the multitude offered.'

Leffingwell saw the office as fertile ground in which to sow the gospel according to Taylor. He published frequently in the monthly magazine *System* (founded in 1901, the forerunner of

Business Week), and brought out the first of several books, *Scientific Office Management*, in 1917. His verbose texts covered in minute detail the arrangement of desks to optimise work flow, the distance walked by clerks to reach the water fountain, the design of forms, and even the 'one best way' to open a letter. They remained influential for decades: the third edition of his *Textbook of Office Management* appeared in 1950, three years after his death. Business historians have not been slow to point out the irony that scientific management itself increased the bureaucratic workload through generating forms to be filled, activities to be monitored, and reports to be analysed and filed.

In 1919 Leffingwell founded the National Office Managers' Association, creating a forum for research, debate and discussion. Its regular publications added to the prolific literature on the subject. Meanwhile, in the United Kingdom, the Office Machinery Users' Association, founded in 1915, picked up the importance of giving system precedence over technology and renamed itself the Office Management Association.

Efficiency had long been a priority at Lyons, and the factories were organised very much according to the principles of Taylorism. Each was laid out to handle the particular kind of cake, pie, bun, loaf or bread roll in which it specialised. Under the direction of a Planning Office, every operation was time-and-motion studied to arrive at a fair, efficient time. These times were used both to calculate the number of staff required, and to compute the standard cost of the labour entailed in making the product, which in turn partly determined its selling price. The Lyons company secretary George Booth was interested in extending the same scientific approach to the clerical work of the company. He decided that the best way to find those with the skills to introduce such methods was to venture into graduate recruitment. None of the family board members had been to university, all following their fathers into the business at the earliest opportunity. The usual career path was a spell in the Trocadero kitchens, followed almost

George Booth, Lyons company secretary.

immediately by promotion to the management of one or other of the company's businesses – tea, confectionery or hotels, for example. While some prided themselves on their ability to add up a column of figures rapidly and accurately, they had no experience of mathematical analysis or scientific enquiry. Below general management level in Lyons the usual approach was to recruit school leavers and train them for specific tasks. Academic qualifications had hitherto seemed irrelevant.

In 1923 Booth persuaded the board to add some intellectual rigour to the company's management by recruiting some of the brightest young minds in the country. One of the five young men who constituted this new class of management trainee was John

Simmons, who had just received a first-class degree in mathematics from Cambridge. It could have been a risky experiment: brilliant mathematicians do not always make good managers (some have been notoriously incapable of tying their shoelaces). Nonetheless, either by luck or judgement, in John Simmons Booth had found exactly the person he needed.

Born in Ceylon (now Sri Lanka) in 1902, John Richardson Mainwaring Simmons was the son and grandson of missionaries who dedicated their lives to spreading the Christian gospel in the Indian subcontinent. His mother died when he was only five. Two years later his father remarried, to a colleague in the Church Missionary Society. A boy of outstanding intellectual gifts, in 1920 John Simmons entered the University of Cambridge to read mathematics, and emerged three years later with first-class honours. At the time his choice of a career in a catering company was somewhat unexpected for a wrangler, the honorific title of Cambridge's top mathematics graduates. It was even less expected that a company such as Lyons would regard pure mathematics as relevant to its day-to-day activities, beyond the basic task of accurate accounting. Yet Lyons had always been open to progressive ideas in managing its manufacturing operations; it was not hard for Booth to persuade the board that they needed to be equally progressive on the clerical side.

Simmons was unobtrusive in appearance; of medium height and build, he always dressed soberly in a jacket and tie. His hair was neatly combed straight back from his high forehead; his expression was habitually serious but even as a young man he carried an air of absolute conviction. He arrived at Cadby Hall knowing little of business. Nothing in his pious childhood or his years of intellectual endeavour at Cambridge had prepared him for the reality of life at Lyons. On his arrival he was put to work in a department where black-coated clerks still stood at Dickensian high desks entering figures in huge ledgers by hand. Typewriters and adding machines had been introduced into some Lyons departments before 1900 but there had been no serious attempt to rationalise office methods.

A quiet, austere and intellectually exacting man, Simmons found his spiritual home at Lyons; he was to remain with the company for forty-five years. Taken on in the junior role of statistician and management trainee, he nevertheless reported directly to Booth and so had unprecedented access to the highest levels of the Lyons management. Booth gave him a free hand to investigate clerical operations at Lyons and make recommendations. He immediately began to apply his analytical skills to the task of increasing efficiency through eliminating duplication and any unnecessary paperwork. He looked for rational alternatives to methods that had evolved in more or less ad hoc fashion. He streamlined and simplified, breaking jobs down into their component parts and allocating tasks to specialised clerks. He extended the use of office machines wherever they made economic sense.

His top-down approach – analysing the work of the clerks and then telling them how to do it better – owed a great deal to the examples of Taylor and Leffingwell, but he soon found that his mentors had underestimated the human factor. For example, Lyons had three central clerical departments: Accounts, which kept the basic records of incomings and outgoings and managed the payroll; the Stock Department, which kept stock records and computed the costs of producing and distributing Lyons products so that they could be priced accurately; and the Checking Department, which checked the cash takings of the catering establishments against the waitresses' bills. These departments kept records that were intended only for the general managers on the board. The managers of the individual departments – Bakeries, Teashops and so on – had their own offices and kept separate records for their own purposes.

Simmons initially favoured greater centralisation, and began by trying to bring all clerical work into the three main specialist departments. But he very quickly learned that 'arguments which

applied to machines did not necessarily appeal to human beings' –
a lesson that devotees of scientific management often had to learn
the hard way. Imagine his chagrin when he discovered that one
departmental manager, deprived of his personal platoon of clerks
and told to get the information he needed from the central departments, had simply recreated his original office within a year of the
change. Simmons ruefully admitted that 'records had better be
kept where they were going to be used, even if it meant they were
kept somewhat less efficiently'.

Other innovations proved more durable. Simmons saw that
office machines, such as adding and bookkeeping machines,
brought advantages in terms of accuracy and efficiency. There was
a problem, however. The American machines were designed to
work with the decimal system, suitable for US dollars and cents.
The Britain of the 1920s (and indeed for almost fifty years afterwards) used the idiosyncratically non-decimal pounds, shillings and
pence of sterling currency. Moreover, weights and measures each
had their own units, none of them decimal. In 1928 Simmons
solved the problem by training the clerks to convert currency and
weights and measures into decimal units before carrying out calculations on the machines, and then back again afterwards. Five years
later a textbook, *Office Practice*, by William Campbell, described this
innovation as what was 'usually' done.

True to his ancestry, Simmons went about his work with a
missionary zeal. The company was supportive of his incremental
reforms, but after a few years he felt he needed to establish the
scientific approach to management on a more permanent basis.
The board agreed to let him set up a department of Systems
Research within Lyons – a team of analysts who would investigate
inefficiencies and bottlenecks in the company's office systems
and propose solutions. A forerunner of what was later called the
Organisation and Methods Department, it was one of the first
such research departments in the country. Once it was up and
running Simmons recruited a twenty-four-year-old chartered

secretary called Geoffrey Mills to manage it. Mills quickly became an effective evangelist for Simmons's scientific approach, and later published a series of textbooks on office management. Up to this point British authors had been slow to follow the American consultant William Henry Leffingwell's lead in providing the tools to educate a new generation of managers. Mills's first book, *Office Organization and Method* (1949) was dedicated to John Simmons and acknowledged his 'authoritative criticism and advice'. It referred to Leffingwell's textbooks, but at the same time echoed Simmons's own mature reflection on the limits of the scientific approach to running an office. 'The clerks . . . are often the most difficult to understand. It is they who make office management an art as well as a science.'

Mills was the architect of another innovation, audacious in its simplicity, that lightened the load on Lyons's clerical systems by using a new technology to make paperwork unnecessary. In 1935 Systems Research received a plea for help from the Wholesale Bakery Sales Department, which supplied bread and cakes directly to shops all over the country. They found that clerks were drowning in paper, copies of invoices and packing notes, all of which needed to be filed. By using an early microfilm camera, called a Recordak, to make the only record of customers' orders, they were able to use the same paper order for pricing and valuation, then as a packing list and eventually to return it to the customer as an invoice, leaving nothing to file. It was the first commercial use of microfilm anywhere in the world.

Though they did not know it at the time, the questions Simmons's young disciples in Systems Research set out to ask, and the analyses they produced – accompanied by beautifully drawn flow charts – were exactly those that would confront businesses two decades later as they grappled with the possibilities of computers in the office.

Simmons's zeal for reform won him notice well beyond Lyons. In 1933 he became a member of the Office Management

Association. A year later he was on the governing council, and by 1938 he was chairman, a post he held until 1950. The Association's members included representatives of most of the major British industrial and commercial firms, and it regularly held conferences to discuss advances in methods and technology. Simmons, with the confidence born of absolute conviction, placed himself in the vanguard of this movement. If there was anyone in the country who had the experience and vision to recognise what computers could do for a business, it was him.

2

The Electronic Brain

John Simmons was a hard man to convince. Here in his office were two of his most trusted lieutenants, Oliver Standingford and Raymond Thompson, babbling excitedly about an 'electronic brain' and asking his permission to visit a military research laboratory in the United States to find out what was going on in the field of electronic, digital computing in the aftermath of the Second World War. They seemed to think an electronic calculator might be relevant to their mission to increase clerical efficiency. Yes, he conceded, like them he had always dreamed of automating routine office work. But in 1946, with an exhausted economy and severe currency restrictions in force, it was absurd to think of buying an expensive American machine, even if such a machine existed.

Not that Simmons was opposed to the American trip itself; it had been his idea to send the two men across the Atlantic as soon as possible after the war was over to find out about the latest developments in office machines and office methods. The American office technology industry had virtually no counterpart in the United Kingdom, apart from its own licensed offshoots, and Simmons had long been used to monitoring American innovations as he developed his own approach to office management. He had made his own first visit to the United States, as a young trainee in 1925, to find out how big companies there managed their operations.

One of the companies Simmons had visited on that occasion was International Business Machines. IBM traced its origins to the invention of punched card calculators by a young New York engineer named Herman Hollerith at the end of the previous century. While working for the Bureau of the Census in Washington DC, Hollerith had invented a range of machines that could process the data from census returns by means of holes punched in cards. Hollerith's innovation was so much faster than manual methods that it seemed little short of miraculous at the time. It received its first trial in the analysis of the 1890 US census. Clerks entered each citizen's details on a single card, about the size of an elongated postcard, which was printed with a 40-column grid of numbers. By hitting a key on a keyboard corresponding to a particular position on the grid, the operator punched a hole in the card: the positions of the holes represented the citizen's age, sex, employment category and so on. The stacks of cards were then fed into a 'tabulating machine'. The machine sensed the positions of the holes through a matching matrix of spring-loaded pins, each of which completed an electrical circuit if it passed through a hole and thereby added one digit to the running total in one of the forty counters operating concurrently in the machine. Another type of machine called a sorter could arrange the cards in alphabetical or numerical order. With dozens of machines operating at once, Hollerith had a rough population count ready within six weeks, and detailed analysis of the results in just over two years. By contrast, the 1880 census, analysed with pencil and paper by almost 1,500 clerks, had taken seven years to complete.

Hollerith quickly saw the commercial possibilities of his machines, and after forming his Tabulating Machine Company in 1896 he successfully sold a number of installations to factories, insurance companies, telephone companies and other large businesses. In failing health, in 1911 he finally agreed to sell his company to a wealthy investor, Charles Ranlegh Flint, for $2.3 million. Flint merged the company with the Computing Scale Company, which made scales for shopkeepers, and the International Time Recording Company, which made the clocks that employees punched as they arrived and left their workplaces each day. The new company was called C-T-R (the Computing-Tabulating-Recording Company) and Flint appointed Thomas J. Watson Sr as general manager.

Watson had developed his consummate skills as a salesman in the aggressive culture of the National Cash Register Company (NCR). He quickly rose to the position of sales manager there, but was summarily fired in 1911 by the company's eccentric founder John H. Patterson. On his arrival at C-T-R he immediately implemented many of the marketing and sales strategies he had learned at NCR, rapidly transforming it into a key player in the office machines business in the first decades of the twentieth century. Under Watson it was the company's practice to lease its machines rather than selling them outright, ensuring a continuing income even in times when new customers were hard to find. It also held a monopoly on the supply of the cards. By 1924 the company had subsidiaries operating across four continents and in that year, to reflect its increasingly global impact, Watson changed its name to International Business Machines – IBM.

The following year, when John Simmons arrived from Lyons to pay a visit, the young Englishman had not found it difficult to resist the hard sell. To hire the machines and buy the specially made cards was expensive, and for the purposes of Lyons, the time and labour needed to punch the cards and feed them through the machine was not much less than that needed to do the work manually. Simmons judged the application of this technology to be of little relevance to the clerical administration of Lyons's food manufacturing and distribution business. At that time he was more interested in extending his company's use of manual adding and accounting machines, and in introducing the kind of office organisation extolled by American authors such as Leffingwell.

According to Oliver Standingford's own account, when he and Thompson went to the United States in 1947 it was he who proposed that their research should include an enquiry into electronic computers. Standingford had joined Lyons straight from school in 1930 as a management trainee in the Stock Department. By that time, Simmons's reforms had included a new system of cost accounting that included setting rigorous standards for every step in the food production chain. Everything was specified, from the value of the energy needed to bake a loaf of bread to the thickness of the jam spread on the Swiss rolls. Much of the clerical work in the Stock Department involved checking actual performance against these standards. It was a task that produced useful information for management but was short on job-satisfaction for most of the clerks who had to carry it out. Standingford had found himself supervising a section of 'seventy calculator operators doing nothing but multiplying, adding, subtracting and writing down the answers by hand'.

Although he was no engineer, Standingford had looked at the technology around him and had begun to think about how it might be used to automate the work of the Stock Department clerks. Towards the end of the 1930s, he had come up with a scheme for 'a device composed of the existing multiplying accounting machine and an arrangement of automatic telephone equipment and magnetic records ... It would have stored information and recovered it automatically.' Eager for the endorsement of a more technically minded supporter, he had shown his plans to Jack Edwards, Lyons's chief electrical engineer. The most Edwards had been prepared to concede was that the idea was 'not mad'.

With war in Europe becoming inevitable, there was no opportunity to take it further. Both Standingford and Edwards had signed up for war service and would not return to Lyons until 1945. As soon as the war was over, Edwards had sought out Standingford, having never forgotten the eager young manager's questions. In the course of his war service as an engineer, Edwards had discovered that the military boffins had developed electronic devices to improve the aim of the anti-aircraft gunners who had successfully defended British skies. Electronics, he suggested, would be the technology of the future for office machines, much faster than the electromechanical machines then in use.

The field of electronics was launched almost a century ago with the invention of the thermionic valve (or vacuum tube as it is known in the United States). First invented by the British scientist John Ambrose Fleming in 1904, a valve looks like a small light bulb. It consists of a glass tube from which all the air has been removed, sealed to maintain the vacuum inside. Held upright, side by side within the tube, is a small number of metal wires, or electrodes. Fleming's original invention had just two electrodes and so was known as a diode; later models incorporated up to five electrodes. Just as the valve in a plumbing system holds back water until someone opens it by turning a tap, thermionic valves allow current to flow in one direction only. They had revolutionised radio engineering during the 1920s, valve-based receivers replacing the crystal sets that had first been used to capture broadcasts. Edwards explained to Standingford that a calculating device made of valves would be thousands of times faster than any mechanical design as it would have no moving parts: all of its operations would be carried out by the movement of electrons in wires.

Standingford had hardly digested this information when he saw an article reporting that American engineers at the Moore School of Engineering at the University of Pennsylvania in Philadelphia had developed just such a machine, which the article described as an 'electronic brain'. He was immensely excited at this development, and determined to investigate further.

In the post-war reorganisation of Lyons, John Simmons had been appointed comptroller. This somewhat archaic title referred in Lyons to the head of management accounting – the person responsible for presenting the company's figures to the board in such a way that managers could identify areas for action and improvement. The Comptroller's Department gradually assumed overall responsibility for the management of clerical work in the other departments. Standingford was promoted to become one of the assistant comptrollers. It was in this capacity that Simmons proposed to send him to the United States, in May 1947, to study advances in office methods. Accompanying him on the trip would be Simmons's chief protégé, Raymond Thompson. Sensing that he would have an able advocate in Thompson, Standingford sounded him out before the two of them approached Simmons to ask permission to visit the Moore School while they were in the United States. He was more successful that he could have hoped – Simmons later insisted to an interviewer that it was Thompson's idea to investigate computers.

Thomas Raymond Thompson had been recruited by Simmons to further his ideas for Lyons. In May 1931 he had written to Simmons on his own initiative. 'Being up in Town for a few days, I am venturing to call and see you on Tuesday,' he began. 'I am looking for a position as Secretary, Assistant Secretary, Accountant or Statistician of a progressive business and I thought it possible that you might have some such position to offer me.' Simmons's reputation had evidently travelled far; for the previous two years Thompson had been working as acting secretary to a Liverpool department store, Owen Owen. Born in 1907 into a relatively humble family – his father ran a grocer's shop – he won a scholarship to Cambridge where, like Simmons, he proved to be one of the ablest mathematicians of his generation and graduated with first-class honours.

There the similarity between the two men ended. While Simmons was soft-spoken and unfailingly courteous, Thompson was excitable, choleric and arrogant. Where Simmons spoke and wrote with thoughtful elegance, choosing his phrases carefully and striving for clarity, Thompson's enthusiasm at times ran ahead of his powers of expression, so that the words tumbled out with little sense of whether his listeners were keeping up. He was given to explosions of temper if he believed that subordinates were slacking, or if crossed in argument, and was universally known (behind his back) by his initials TRT, no doubt for their resemblance to the explosive TNT. He grasped new ideas with great rapidity and was full of what one of his acquaintances described as 'intellectual joy', a quality that could be appealing as long as you were not on the receiving end of one of his wrathful outbursts. Simmons, for whom the younger man had enormous respect, was able to channel Thompson's enthusiasm and harness his undoubted ability. In 1947 Thompson had just been appointed chief assistant comptroller, and so was the more senior of the two men making the trip to the United States.

At the time the post-war shortage of labour had to some extent lessened the burden of clerical work at Lyons. The company had shared the indomitable spirit of wartime London, serving tea in its surviving teashops (70 were destroyed by bombs) throughout the Blitz and entertaining soldiers on leave with the gaiety of its Corner Houses. Part of Cadby Hall, which survived unbombed, became a depot where volunteers packed boxes of rations to be dispatched to serving soldiers. Many Lyons staff at all levels either joined the services or took up war-related work elsewhere. One group of Lyons managers even ran a munitions factory at Elstree. With exemplary efficiency, the factory had turned out millions of bombs by the time the war was over.

The vast majority of Lyons staff who had been on active service returned to their old jobs in 1945. The post-war picture was subtly altered, however. One symptom of the harsher climate was that the Nippies had disappeared from the teashops. Labour shortages in wartime had forced Lyons to convert the shops to self-service cafeterias, and when the war ended, rising costs obliged the company to keep the same system. No waitresses in the teashops meant no Checking Department – the job for which John Simmons had dreamed of using a miraculous automatic machine had simply ceased to exist. But his vision had fired the imagination of his younger colleagues: 'the idea,' as Simmons later put it to an interviewer, 'was in our blood'.

Yet Simmons himself was at first surprisingly lukewarm about

Standingford's plan to look at computers in the United States. Being unaware of any moves towards electronic computing in the United Kingdom, he assumed that the only way to acquire a machine of the 'electronic brain' variety would be to buy it from an American supplier, and it was virtually impossible for British firms to spend such large sums of money overseas at the time. But before he finally came to a decision he consulted his mentor, the ageing company secretary George Booth. Booth expressed the indulgent view that 'youth should be given its head, even if that head contains unusual ideas'. (At the time Standingford was thirty-seven and Thompson forty, but such things are relative: Booth was seventy-eight.)

So Simmons wrote to Dr Herman Goldstine, a researcher then at the maths and science hothouse, the Institute for Advanced Study in Princeton, asking if Thompson and Standingford might come and see him. During the war Goldstine had been the US army liaison officer attached to the Moore School of Engineering in Philadelphia, where the 'electronic brain' – or to give it its proper name, the Electronic Numerical Integrator and Computer, ENIAC – had been developed for the US Army Ballistics Research Laboratory. He replied that the two men would be welcome to visit him. In the spring of 1947 (a spring all the more welcome in that it followed one of the worst British winters in living memory), Thompson and Standingford boarded a ship for the five-day crossing of the Atlantic.

It brought them to a land of plenty, even of excess: abundant food, central heating, large, gas-guzzling automobiles, all in stark contrast to the privations of bombed-out, rationed Britain. But they were far from dazzled by much of what they saw. In the course of a whirlwind programme of visits to office equipment suppliers and large organisations, they found nothing to match the systems that had been put in place at Lyons by Simmons and his team. They were astonished at the readiness of American managers to have their problems diagnosed by office machinery salesmen, whose remedies inevitably involved buying more of their equipment. Few seemed to have paid more than lip-service to the ideal of scientific management, apparently happy to believe that efficiency could be bought off the shelf from whichever salesman produced the most convincing argument or dazzling demonstration. For example, most companies were using IBM's punched-card installations, but few had seriously evaluated their cost-effectiveness.

Even in the layout of office buildings, Thompson and Standingford felt that the new Lyons administrative building at Cadby Hall, Elms House, meticulously designed under John Simmons's direction according to the principles of scientific management, was superior to any American organisation's offices. While they were in Washington DC they took in the War Department's Pentagon office building, completed only three years before at a cost of $80 million. Their guide reeled off the statistics: 30,000 workers, more than 6.5 million square feet of floor space on five floors, and 17½ miles of corridors. The two men left, laughing and shaking their heads incredulously at the time that would be wasted in getting from one part of the building to another.

At last they headed for Princeton and their meeting with Herman Goldstine – a meeting that made the whole trip worthwhile.

ENIAC

Herman Goldstine was the godfather of ENIAC, the 'electronic brain' that had caused such a fever of press excitement and had stimulated Raymond Thompson and Oliver Standingford to explore the possibilities of electronic computing. Having gained a PhD in mathematics from the University of Chicago, Goldstine joined the army when the United States entered the war. In 1942 he found himself assigned to the army's Ballistics Research Laboratory at the Aberdeen Proving Ground in Maryland, with the rank of lieutenant. In his crisp uniform he looked every inch the military man, but he never truly left academic life behind; always hungry for ideas, when he found a good one he would do everything possible to make sure it had a chance to flourish.

One of his tasks was to liaise with the Moore School of Engineering, not far away in Philadelphia. Here, teams of women – 'human computors' – were being trained to calculate firing tables for artillery using mechanical desk calculators. With ordnance capable of firing along parabolic trajectories over a range of up to a mile, it was impossible for heavy gunners to take accurate aim by eye. The tables told the gunners how high to aim their weapons given a target at a certain range, calculated on the basis of the weight of the shell, its velocity on leaving the muzzle, and other variables such as the wind speed and direction, and the air temperature and density. A typical trajectory required 750 multiplications, and a typical firing table about 3,000 trajectories. Goldstine was desperate for an alternative to these human computers, whose work was time-consuming and vulnerable to error.

He found what he was looking for in a proposal to build an 'electronic computor' (*sic*) containing 5,000 valves, put forward in 1942 by John Mauchly, a physicist trained for war-related work in electronics at the Moore School. The army refused to take the proposal seriously until Goldstine took up Mauchly's cause in the spring of 1943 and, through careful diplomacy and a persuasive manner, won from his superiors funding for an even larger revised version. Mauchly was not a great salesman for his own ideas, but was one of very few people in the world at that time who grasped the potential of electronics in computing. Before the war he had worked on the design of a (non-electronic) machine to automate numerical methods of weather forecasting. Through giving a talk on this work he had met John Atanasoff, a professor at Iowa State College, who invited him to see his own prototype computer. It was an electronic adder – properly a calculator rather than a computer – with a modest 300 valves, which Atanasoff had built with his graduate student Clifford Berry between 1939 and 1942.

Mauchly had spent five days discussing it, although he later denied that he had learned anything from Atanasoff. The work had received virtually no recognition at the time, and never advanced beyond a working prototype. But the priority of the little Atanasoff-Berry Computer (ABC) was established years later in a successful bid to deny patents on aspects of the ENIAC design to the Moore School team. The question 'who invented the computer?' still rages on internet sites and in a succession of publications, and probably does not have a clear answer. Credit for being the first to build a valve-based prototype calculating machine should probably be shared between Atanasoff and Berry, and Konrad Zuse and Helmut Schreyer, who built an electronic demonstration model at the Technical University in Berlin in 1938.

Whatever it owed to his encounter with John Atanasoff, John Mauchly's proposal exceeded anything previously seen in its scope and ambition. ENIAC, conceived by Mauchly but brought to life by teams of engineers working sixteen-hour days under the direction of the gifted Moore School engineer Presper Eckert, was a monster. As eventually completed in 1945, it was 2.5 metres high and nearly 50 metres long, its racks of valves, cables and other components arranged in a U-shape around the walls of a large room. It weighed over 30 tons, incorporated almost 18,000 valves, and cost the army $800,000. When it was working, ENIAC could perform 14 10-digit multiplications a second – 500 times faster than the best of the female 'computors' with their mechanical machines.

Its reliability, however, was in inverse proportion to its size: the only certain thing about its performance was that it would break down at least once a day. Valves, like light bulbs, have a limited life, and losing just one out of the 18,000 could ruin a calculation. More serious shortcomings were built into its design. Its builders could have cut the number of valves by over a third if they had considered representing the data in the machine in binary code.

Human calculators, having ten fingers, find it easiest to do arithmetic using decimal numbers. For computers, however, it makes much more sense to use the binary system. Binary code resembles Morse code in that it has only two symbols, usually written as 0 and 1. Any number can be converted into its unique binary equivalent – a string of 0s and 1s in which the value of each place is twice the value of its right-hand neighbour, rather than ten times as much as in the decimal system:

Decimal	Binary	Decimal	Binary
1	1	11	1011
2	10	12	1100
3	11	13	1101
4	100	14	1110
5	101	15	1111
6	110	16	10000
7	111	17	10001
8	1000	18	10010
9	1001	19	10011
10	1010	20	10100

The advantage for computers of thinking in binary code is that their language consists of identical electrical pulses. At any point in a circuit, either there is a pulse, or there is not. On or off. 1 or 0. While a message written out in binary code might look extraordinarily cumbersome, it is in fact much quicker for a computer to work with instructions in this form than to incorporate some more complicated method of representing all the numbers and letters that human brains cope with quite happily.

In ENIAC, Eckert and Mauchly represented numbers in their conventional decimal notation. They used ten valves to represent a single digit: the fifth valve in a row of ten indicated the number five, and so on. Using binary code, just five valves would have been enough to represent all the numbers up to 31. To be fair to the Moore School designers, the theory of information processing based on binary digits, or 'bits' for short, was still being developed by Claude Shannon at Bell Labs when they began work on ENIAC. It has since been fundamental to the design of all modern computers.

Another major shortcoming of ENIAC was that it could not store programs. Mauchly had not taken the logical step that as programs consisted of information that could be represented digitally, they could be treated in the same way as data and stored in the computer itself. Each time ENIAC's engineers wanted to run a new calculation they had to set up the program afresh by plugging wires into sockets, a process that could take a whole day.

The machine's own builders realised that by the time they had it working, it was already obsolete. It deserves credit, however, for being the first to demonstrate publicly the power of electronic computing. It did work for the purpose for which it had been designed, and the army went on using it until 1955. Meanwhile, the publicity it attracted stimulated others to develop new avenues in the history of computing that would lead directly to the computers of today.

Among those who watched the building of ENIAC with interest was the Hungarian émigré mathematician John von Neumann. Von Neumann was by then an international star of mathematics, having established the mathematical foundations of quantum theory as well as developing the principles of game theory, which were to have a huge impact in economics, international relations, population biology and many other areas of modern experience. He was a founder member of the Institute for Advanced Study in Princeton, and had become an adviser to the army in 1940 when he joined the scientific advisory committee of its Ballistics Research Laboratory. Since 1943 he had also been attached to the Los Alamos atomic bomb project. At that time he was trying to model the explosion of the bomb mathematically and to predict the ensuing fireball, but had not been able to find any machine capable of crunching the numbers fast enough.

According to Herman Goldstine's widely circulated account, it was his own chance meeting with von Neumann that first brought ENIAC to the renowned mathematician's attention. One day in 1944 Goldstine looked up while waiting on a station platform for a train from Aberdeen to Philadelphia and saw von Neumann just a few feet away. Conscious of his lowly academic status but never one to miss an opportunity, he introduced himself and they fell into conversation. When the topic turned to ENIAC and what it would be able to do, Goldstine remembered, 'the whole atmosphere changed from one of relaxed good humor to one more like the oral examination for the doctor's degree in mathematics'.

A few months later von Neumann became a consultant to the Moore School team on the design of a successor machine that would avoid the serious shortcomings that had become apparent as ENIAC came into operation. Called the Electronic Discrete Variable Automatic Computer (EDVAC), it would handle data more economically by using binary rather than decimal digits and, most important of all, it would incorporate the means to store programs along with data.

In June 1945 von Neumann summarised these discussions in a memo, 'A First Draft of a Report on the EDVAC', formalising the logical design of such a machine. The report described the principles of an automatic, digital machine, consisting of five basic components: a memory, which stores both program and data; a control unit, which interprets the program; an arithmetic unit, which adds and subtracts data as directed by the program; and input and output units, which read in the program and data and deliver the final results. Computers with this design – and that includes the vast majority of modern computers – have ever since been said to have 'von Neumann architecture'.

As in the case of Atanasoff and Mauchly, much ink and hot air has been expended over the injustice done to Eckert and Mauchly in denying them credit, especially for the stored program concept. Eckert had not only thought about this before John von Neumann joined the project; he had begun to design and build a prototype store. There was undoubtedly a conflict of interest between the academics von Neumann and Goldstine, who wanted to see the ideas in the EDVAC design incorporated as widely as possibly, and the engineers Eckert and Mauchly, who were thinking about capitalising on its commercial possibilities. The academics won hands down when Goldstine, apparently on his own initiative, distributed the report with von Neumann's sole name on it to a couple of dozen carefully selected recipients. That was all it took to ensure that von Neumann's name was permanently cemented to the concept of a stored program. Although EDVAC itself, eventually delivered to the Aberdeen Proving Ground in 1949, was not an especially significant machine, every subsequent computer designer was influenced by the contents of von Neumann's report.

When Oliver Standingford and Raymond Thompson came to see him in 1947, Goldstine was back in academic life. His boldness in accosting John von Neumann on that station platform had paid off, and he was now working as his assistant on a new computer project at the Institute for Advanced Study. The two men found him in his office on the elegant, tree-shaded campus. His mood was relaxed and expansive. If he was surprised at being approached by representatives of a commercial company, far from the world of theoretical physics and higher mathematics that he inhabited, he gave no sign of it. He listened closely as the two men explained that they were exploring the possibility of using electronic calculators in the office. 'That's not a problem I've thought about before,' began Goldstine. Thompson eagerly explained how much of the work of the Lyons clerks amounted to routine calculation, and how their whole approach to office systems was based on distilling useful information from the mass of data.

Goldstine instantly saw the point, and became tremendously enthusiastic. Sketching furiously on a yellow pad, he launched into a description of possible approaches to the problem given the technology that had been developed so far. At the same time he explained the advantages of electronic calculators of the type he was now working on over previous types of calculating machine. The most obvious was their speed of operation. While an IBM punched card tabulator could carry out the same processes of addition and subtraction, its speed was limited by the speed of its mechanical moving parts. The electronic calculator, in contrast, operated at the speed of an electron moving in space – in principle, each step in a calculation could be completed in less than a millionth of a second.

The real source of an electronic calculator's power, said Goldstine, was its potential to store its own program along with interim and final results. It would operate automatically – there was little or no need for human intervention in the course of a run. While punched card machines could carry out as many parallel operations as there were columns on the card (the standard had increased from 40 to 80 since Hollerith's time), most electronic computers operated serially, taking one instruction or piece of data from the store at a time. However, the gain in speed and the possibility of running a large number of different operations in a single program gave the electronic computer overwhelming superiority.

Goldstine finished by giving Thompson and Standingford a list of everyone he knew about in the United States who was doing serious work on electronic computing. Then, enjoying the astonishment of his listeners, he dropped his bombshell. 'And, of course, there's Professor Douglas Hartree in Cambridge, England.'

Hartree had recently been appointed Professor of Mathematical Physics at Cambridge University. Goldstine informed his astonished listeners that one of Hartree's new colleagues was building a state-of-the-art computer in the Mathematical Laboratory there. The two men had come 3,000 miles to find out that a computer was already under construction a couple of hours' drive away from Lyons's headquarters. Goldstine warmly recommended that Thompson and Standingford should talk to Hartree about their ideas for a business computer. As soon as they had left, he sat down and dispatched a letter to Cambridge on their behalf.

With a much clearer understanding of the technology, and buoyed up by Goldstine's enthusiasm, Thompson and Standingford then made a tour of every organisation on his list. They were not able to see ENIAC itself, which had been taken over by the army and was being rebuilt at their Aberdeen firing range. Permission initially granted was suddenly withdrawn on the grounds of confidentiality – but Goldstine said later that the army's engineers had probably failed to get the notoriously unreliable machine working and were too embarrassed to admit it. At the Moore School itself, where ENIAC had been built in a spirit of adventure and enthusiasm, they found that the disbanding of the original team had left 'a general air of apathy'. A smaller experimental calculator was built and working, but no one showed the smallest interest in their ideas on office computing.

Presper Eckert and John Mauchly, who had designed and built ENIAC, had left the Moore School a year earlier (following a dispute with Goldstine and von Neumann about the right to patent their invention) to form the Electronic Control Company. They, apparently alone among the early computer pioneers, planned to develop a computer for commercial production based on the EDVAC design, to be known as the Universal Automatic Calculator or UNIVAC. Naturally, a visit to their Philadelphia office was high on Thompson and Standingford's list of priorities.

Eckert told them that he was talking to the Prudential Insurance Company of America about designing a machine to issue bills, and to carry out actuarial calculations. The big insurance companies had millions of policyholders and employed thousands of clerks to draft policies and send out bills for premiums. The office machinery suppliers had come up with some labour-saving devices for this kind of work, such as machines for printing frequently used addresses, but essentially the insurance business required heroic efforts of typing and filing. Prudential was the first and only example Thompson and Standingford came across of a company planning to use a computer for clerical work. A visit to its offices in Newark, New Jersey, revealed a company with an attitude as progressive as that of Lyons, though in a completely different line of business. It had a large Methods Division (comparable to the Systems Research Department at Lyons), with an innovator at its head, Dr Edmund C. Berkeley (later to become the author of the first popular computing book, *Giant Brains*). He was apparently confident that his company would have a machine installed and working within two years. In addition to preparing bills for insurance premiums, Berkeley planned to use the machine to prepare contracts, storing the 2,000 standard clauses and programming the machine to select those required in individual cases. This was the first Thompson and Standingford had heard of the possibilities computers offered for what we now call word processing. As things turned out, the Electronic Control Company was dogged by financial problems; in 1950 Prudential cancelled its contract with Eckert and Mauchly and later bought its first computer from IBM.

Extraordinary as it seems today, Eckert and Mauchly were out on a limb in perceiving a need for a general purpose commercial computer which could be produced for sale. The obvious candidates to pursue such a development were the existing office machine companies, who already had the customers and the sales forces to exploit a new market. Those that the Lyons pair visited, such as IBM, NCR and Burroughs, were secretive about their own research but they seemed to be more concerned to protect their traditional products than to develop entirely new ones. Standingford later wrote: 'We were given a polite hearing, lunch and the sort of restrained reception reserved for the mentally unstable.'

It was a relief to have their confidence restored with a second visit to Goldstine. They found he had spent the intervening weeks thinking about the special requirements of office computing, and he gave them a detailed list of the components their computer would need. This time he took them to his engineering labs and showed them not only his partly built computer but prototype peripherals such as a device that would load programs and data into the machine through spinning magnetic wire (a forerunner of magnetic tape) from one reel to another. Profuse in their gratitude for Goldstine's information and encouragement, Thompson and Standingford returned to New York and the boat home in a state of intellectual euphoria. Their minds were ablaze with the possibilities before them. While some might have used the cruise home, on the *Queen Elizabeth*, as an opportunity to relax, they lost no time in recording the knowledge and impressions they had gained in the first draft of the lengthy report on their visit they would be presenting to the Lyons board.

The first three sections of the report disposed of their visits to office machine companies and other businesses, concluding that Lyons's methods were already so advanced that they had little to learn in this sphere. But Section D, headed 'Electronic Machines in the Office', stands as a prophetic document, showing both a firm grasp of the capabilities and limitations of the technology then developing, and a vision of where it all might lead. It was never published at the time, circulating only within Lyons, but in Britain at least no comparable account of the subject had ever been written.

Thompson and Standingford were unequivocal about their own enthusiasm for an electronic calculating machine. 'Our object,' they wrote, 'in inquiring into the nature and possibilities of this machine was to find out whether it, or any adaptation of it, was capable of being put to use in commercial offices, and if this was not the case, to try to stimulate the development of such a machine.' They went on to list the functions a computer might be capable of performing: storing data and instructions, performing sequences of calculations on stored material automatically, comparing words or figures in its memory and reacting to differences, and printing out results. They emphasised the astonishing speed at which these functions could be carried out, but showed how it posed a problem whose solution would later become the first priority in the development of the Lyons computer. 'It is obviously wasteful to have a machine that is capable of working at these superhuman speeds,' they wrote, 'unless the information it is to work upon can be made available to it at relatively comparable speeds. The feeding clearly cannot be directly by clerks but mechanical and electrical means have been developed that are satisfactory.'

Thompson and Standingford recognised that what might be 'satisfactory' for a computer working on mathematical problems that might require minutes or hours of computation would not do in an office, 'where the problem is to carry out a large number of simple operations'. This note of realism continued in an account of the importance of punching every input tape twice, using a device that compared the first and second versions to eliminate errors. The authors had clearly absorbed the philosophy that time on the computer was valuable, and everything possible had to be done to make sure that it was used efficiently.

After giving a short summary of the memory devices then under development, and an account of how a computer actually worked, Thompson and Standingford went on to suggest three examples of its applications in the office: sales invoicing, the typing of form letters and payroll. In each case, they explained, permanent information such as customers' code numbers and addresses or employees' names and rates of pay could be stored on magnetic wire or teleprinter tape and used again and again, while each week another input tape or wire would be prepared, giving hours worked, bonuses and so on. These two, together with an 'instruction wire' containing the program, would be played into the computer's memory, the necessary calculation performed, and the computer would then print automatically the invoices, letters or payslips required.

Although almost all of their informants had been preoccupied with computers as mathematical tools, Thompson and Standingford were able to use their own background in systems research at Lyons to see how clerical tasks with rather little mathematical content, such as word processing and payroll management, could be recast as 'calculations' for the computer. It was a lateral step that hardly anyone, with the possible exceptions of Eckert and Mauchly and Edmund C. Berkeley at Prudential Insurance, had yet taken. All that now remained was to convince Simmons and the Lyons board that this was the way they should go in the future.

3

Made in Britain

It was predictable that Simmons and his colleagues should look to the United States for advances in technology, including computers. Its vast markets, coupled with a native enthusiasm for innovation, provided a fertile breeding ground for ideas and their commercial development. They did not know at that stage that the history of computing also owed much to British pioneers.

Charles Babbage (1792–1871), a showman as much as a thinker, had been in the forefront of the enthusiasm for scientific discovery and technological invention that ignited elements of London society in the first few decades of the nineteenth century. Although he had held the post of Lucasian Professor of Mathematics at the University of Cambridge for a number of years, he had spent very little time there. He was interested in everything, but his greatest concern was to subject the problems of society to scientific and preferably numerical analysis. He developed a passionate interest in factory management, and the studies he carried out predated by almost a century the 'time and motion' craze of the 1920s and 1930s. For example, in his 1832 book *On the Economy of Machinery and Manufactures* he published figures on the numbers of men, women and children needed to make pins, the time taken for each part of the process and the cost of each pin, taking into account labour and materials.

Writing of his search for laws and principles governing factory work, he commented: 'Having been inclined during the last ten years to visit a considerable number of workshops and factories, both in England and on the Continent, for the purpose of making myself acquainted with the various resources of the mechanical art, I was insensibly led to apply to them those principles of generalisation to which my other pursuits had naturally given rise.' From his observations he developed a poor opinion of the ability of the human species to undertake any repetitive work reliably. 'One of the great advantages which we may derive from machinery,' he said, 'is from the check which it affords against the inattention of, the idleness or the dishonesty of human agents.'

The Industrial Revolution was in full swing. Machines spun and wove in factories at speeds unmatched by traditional cottage industry. Babbage the mathematician began to wonder if a machine could be made to do calculations. The best approach, he soon realised, was to reduce the calculation to a series of simpler stages, so that all the machine had to do was add and subtract. He owed this insight to the French mathematician Gaspard Riche de Prony, who had been charged with finding a feasible way to calculate all the new mathematical tables that would be needed following the introduction of the metric system by the French revolutionary government. De Prony's solution was to organise a hierarchy of mathematical workers, beginning with a few professional mathematicians at the top and ending with a large team, who could add and subtract according to a formula worked out by those higher up the ladder. (The lowest tier was composed of redundant hairdressers, whose former customers had either lost their hair along with their heads, or prudently adopted a style of suitably radical simplicity.)

Babbage was convinced that anything a roomful of hairdressers could do, a machine could do better. He drew up designs for what he called his Difference Engine, and eventually persuaded the government to part with funds for its development. He got as far as producing a demonstration model that he displayed to wondering visitors in his London drawing room. It consisted of dozens of interconnected brass cogs with complex gears between them, which would perform predetermined (and apparently 'miraculous') procedures as he cranked a handle. The money ran out before he could produce a full-scale version. His design was vindicated when in 1991 curators at the Science Museum in London used his notes and drawings to produce his improved Difference Engine No. 2. Doron Swade, who led the project, tells the whole story in his book *The Cogwheel Brain*.

Money was not the only problem. Babbage had sidetracked himself by thinking up an even better machine: the Analytical Engine. Rather than setting up a calculation by positioning various cogs by hand, Babbage proposed to feed the Analytical Engine both program and data on punched cards such as those the French inventor Joseph Marie Jacquard had developed to automate the weaving of damask patterns into cloth. The machine never progressed beyond the design stage (although the design notes filled thirty volumes). But it encompassed much of the thinking behind the design of modern electronic computers: it had inputs, in the form of punched cards, a store or memory, a processing unit (which Babbage called the 'mill'), and a variety of different outputs, including printed results or more card-punching.

The Analytical Engine also inspired a historic document, all the more remarkable in its day because the author was a woman. The document was entitled 'Sketch of the Analytical Engine invented by Charles Babbage Esq.' and published in *Taylor's Scientific Memoirs* in September 1843. The 'Sketch' was originally written in French by the Italian engineer Luigi Menabrea. The English translation in the *Memoirs*, with the addition of extensive explanatory 'Notes', was by Augusta Ada, Countess of Lovelace, and only product of the short-lived marriage between the poet Lord Byron and Annabella Milbanke. Ada Lovelace, who was twenty-eight years old and a mother of three when the 'Sketch' was published, developed a passion for mathematical ideas at an early age. With all the emotional volatility of her father – although a cruelly restricted upbringing could have had as much to do with this as genetics –

her own assessment of her mathematical gifts was sometimes unrealistic. But she formed a strong intellectual bond with Babbage, and proved an able advocate of his work. Her 'Notes' constitute the first accessible description of the capabilities and limitations of a computer. And a century before the sensational 'electronic brain' articles began to appear in the British and American press, she knew better than to oversell the discovery. 'It is desirable,' she wrote, 'to guard against the possibility of exaggerated ideas that might arise as to the powers of the Analytical Engine . . . The Analytical Engine has no pretensions whatever to *originate* any thing. It can do whatever we *know how to order it* to perform . . . Its province is to assist us in making *available*, what we are already acquainted with' (her italics). Today, when commentators frequently speculate that machine intelligence is on the verge of taking over from the human variety, her remark seems as percipient as ever.

Lovelace's 'Notes' are credited with introducing the idea of computer programming, and in 1980 the US Department of Defense named a new programming language 'ADA' in her honour. She also warned that if the British government did not back Babbage's idea, the glory would go elsewhere. Babbage himself felt that his own country greatly undervalued his invention, comparing the English attitude to innovation unfavourably with the American. 'Propose to an Englishman,' he wrote in 1852, 'any principle, or any instrument, however admirable, and you will observe that the whole effort of the English mind is directed to find a difficulty, defect or an impossibility in it . . . Impart the same principle or show the same machine to an American, and you will observe that the whole effort of his mind is to find some new application of the principle, some new use for the instrument.'

It was a lesson that had still to be learned over a century later when the first digital electronic computers began to be built, with British and American engineers running neck and neck. Oliver Standingford and Raymond Thompson were only the latest in a line of British visitors whom Herman Goldstine had briefed on ENIAC since the machine first became public knowledge. In Goldstine's view the computerisation of Great Britain 'owed everything' to what was learned by British visitors to the Moore School in 1945–46. While broadly true, the statement under-estimates what British mathematicians and engineers had already contributed, largely unknown to anyone in the United States. Goldstine was apparently unaware, both when he talked to Thompson and Standingford in 1947 and as late as 1972 when he published his own detailed historical account, that electronic computers had been built and working in Britain while ENIAC had scarcely left the drawing board.

When war broke out, mathematicians and physicists were enlisted to work in British government laboratories and institutions on the development of intelligence and early warning systems that would be vital in the defence of a small country at risk of invasion. Two of the key centres were the Telecommunications Research Establishment (TRE) in Great Malvern, which developed ground-based and airborne radar systems, and the highly secret Government Code and Cipher School at Bletchley Park, codenamed 'Station X'. It was to Bletchley Park, a red-brick country house in Buckinghamshire, surrounded by an encampment of bleak huts, that the mathematician Alan Turing found himself posted.

As a twenty-three-year-old fellow of King's College Cambridge, Turing had published a paper in 1936 that described a class of imaginary computer – or 'Turing machine' as it came to be called. Turing machines operate in a step-by-step, or serial fashion, they can store large amounts of information, and they include a program to direct the order in which operations are carried out. They operate on symbols that are fed to the machine one by one on a tape. Each machine is designed to carry out a particular computation; but a 'Universal Turing Machine' can compute anything that can be computed by any other Turing machine.

Turing developed the hypothetical Turing machine simply as an intellectual tool in the search for an answer to the question of whether a method or process existed that could determine whether any given mathematical assertion was provable. (The answer, he showed definitively, was no.) But while it remains a landmark in pure mathematics, his paper 'On Computable Numbers' is now also credited with containing the first description of the logical structure of a stored-program, digital computer.

When his paper came out, Turing was just beginning a two-year period at the Institute for Advanced Study in Princeton, where John von Neumann was a professor. Turing's biographer Andrew Hodges suggests that von Neumann was slow to recognise the importance of the younger man's paper and Turing, whose social awkwardness meant he often failed to capitalise on opportunities for advancement, did nothing to bring it to his attention. Even so, von Neumann was sufficiently impressed by him to offer him a temporary teaching post. Turing turned the offer down in 1938 in favour of returning to England and his fellowship at King's.

Turing had begun working on codes when he was still at Princeton, and almost immediately on his return to the United Kingdom he was assigned to Bletchley Park. There he joined the team of chess champions, bridge players, crossword fiends and schoolboy mathematicians dedicated to decoding the supposedly unbreakable German radio messages encrypted with the Enigma machine. The machine had a typewriter keyboard and a series of rotors set up in such a way that pressing the letter keys caused different letters to be substituted in the message. In theory the correspondences between the plain text and coded messages could be worked out only if you knew how the rotors had been set before the message was sent – and the rotor settings were changed every day. Just as the Enigma machine mechanised the setting of the codes, the Bletchley Park team needed a machine to work through its thousands of possibilities in order to crack them.

Turing helped to design a code-cracking machine called the

'Bombe'. The Bombe was a special-purpose, electromechanical machine that essentially mimicked several Enigma machines connected together and set up to run automatically. Cracking Enigma codes was never easy, but the Bombe made it possible in a short enough time for the information to be useful. The intelligence Bletchley provided to the British High Command (codenamed 'Ultra') was a vital contribution to the Allied victory in 1945.

It was also from the intellectual hothouse at Bletchley Park that the first true electronic, programmable digital computer emerged, although its existence was a secret for almost thirty years and its designers and builders have only recently received credit for their achievement. Turing and his colleagues needed something special to crack the more complex code used by Hitler himself to communicate with his generals. This code was generated by Lorenz machines. These machines communicated via teleprinter code (patterns of holes punched in paper tape) rather than Morse code, and used a system of almost random 'obscuring characters' to encrypt messages. While the Bletchley code-breakers actually had an Enigma machine in their possession, which Polish allies had managed to appropriate from the Germans before the war, they had never seen a Lorenz machine and did not know its logical structure.

Thanks to a lucky mistake by a pair of German signallers, who sent two versions of the same message using the same settings, the Bletchley team had made some progress towards cracking the Lorenz messages (codenamed 'Fish'). But a single message could take weeks to crack by brainpower alone. The Bletchley mathematicians, Turing among them, called for a machine to automate the statistical analysis of the Fish transmissions. The Bletchley bosses doubted such a thing was possible, but in 1943 Tommy Flowers took away the specification drawn up by Turing's colleague Max Newman and turned it into electronic reality in nine months. Flowers was a naturally gifted engineer who had qualified by putting himself through night school in the 1930s and had risen to a senior position at the Post Office's research centre at Dollis Hill outside London, one of the leading centres of expertise in electronics at the time.

The result was Colossus, a mammoth construction whose power and speed lay in its 1,500 thermionic valves. Colossus could read encoded messages on punched paper tape at 5,000 characters per second, and carry out calculations at previously unimaginable speeds. The heat generated by the valves was so intense that the female operators, drafted in from the Women's Royal Naval Service, were reduced to working in their underwear. Six months later Flowers had built a Mark II Colossus, five times as fast and with 2,500 valves. By the end of the war, Bletchley Park was using ten of these, and the mathematicians were systematically decrypting the German High Command's most secret communications.

The Mark I Colossus, which began work before the end of 1943, is today widely accepted as the world's first full-scale, working, digital electronic computer. Like ENIAC it could not store programs – it was programmed by plugs and switches. Both were evolutionary dead ends in computing terms. It was only ENIAC, however, that provided the impetus for the development of the first stored program computers. The reason is not hard to find. While ENIAC was quickly declassified and achieved worldwide fame in the post-war years, Colossus remained obscured behind the impervious wall of the Official Secrets Act. All the Bletchley Park team, which ran to several thousands over the course of the war, were sworn never to speak of what they had done there. Winston Churchill praised their trustworthiness, calling them 'the geese that laid the golden eggs but never cackled'. On his orders eight of the ten Colossus machines were broken up for Post Office spares as soon as the war ended. The remaining two machines were kept hidden from view at Bletchley Park's successor, the Government Communications Headquarters in Cheltenham, until 1960 when they, too, were destroyed. Tommy Flowers did as he was instructed and burnt all his records.

It was not until 1974, when a former Bletchley Park worker, F. W. Winterbotham, persuaded the authorities that nothing was to be gained from further secrecy, that the achievements of Bletchley Park finally gained public recognition. Winterbotham's book, *The Ultra Secret*, finally made it possible for other Bletchley veterans to talk about matters they had kept secret for thirty years or more, even from their own families. Today the Bletchley Park Trust proudly shows visitors around the site, and a reconstruction of Colossus was unveiled in 1996.

Because of its preoccupation with secrecy, but also because it failed to see the potential, there was no concerted effort on the part of the British government to use the momentum of wartime computing to explore and develop civilian applications. Despite the lack of encouragement, some members of the Bletchley team went on to contribute independently to computer projects in the post-war years. Alan Turing drew up a design for a computer for mathematical work, called the Automatic Computing Engine (ACE), to be built at the National Physical Laboratory in Teddington. John Womersly, who had also been an early British visitor to ENIAC, was head of the newly established mathematics division at NPL. The idea was that the Post Office engineers at Dollis Hill would build the computer to Turing's design, but they had other priorities and the project dragged on. The Pilot ACE was eventually completed in 1951, and subsequently developed by English Electric as the DEUCE.

After differences with Womersly, Turing himself left in 1948 to join the computing laboratory at the University of Manchester. In 1952 he was arrested and charged with gross indecency after admitting a homosexual relationship. The subsequent public humiliation, enforced 'treatment' and withdrawal of his security clearance led to profound depression, which ended with his suicide two years later. Only in recent years, with the publication of several biographies, has his role as a computing pioneer become widely recognised.

Computing on the Cam

British expertise on computing was not wholly confined to Bletchley Park. During the war Douglas Hartree, then a professor of theoretical physics from the University of Manchester, had been in regular contact with the Moore School engineers while working on war-related problem-solving for the British government. They invited him over to advise on ENIAC in 1945, as soon as the European war was over; the following year he stayed in Philadelphia for two months. The computer's job was to find the correct elevation for a particular weapon, given the range and position of the target. The usual method, whether by human 'computor' or machine, was to choose a range of likely elevations and test them one by one, gradually converging on the optimum. Hartree showed the ENIAC designers how to programme the machine so that it would automatically correct after each trial, reaching a solution in a few minutes. 'I do not think it would be an exaggeration,' wrote his biographer, the physicist Sir Charles Darwin, shortly after Hartree's death in 1958, 'to say that it was he who taught them the way in which advantage could be taken of [ENIAC's] extreme rapidity of action.'

In October 1946 Hartree had taken up the post of Professor of Mathematical Physics at the University of Cambridge. As Goldstine informed Thompson and Standingford, his arrival coincided with the start of a highly ambitious project initiated by the University's Mathematical Laboratory: the building of its own electronic computer along the lines set out in von Neumann's 'A First Draft of a Report on the EDVAC'.

In an unusually prescient step for one of the ancient universities, the Cambridge University authorities had set up the Mathematical Laboratory ten years before to provide a computation service to the mathematicians, engineers and scientists of the university's research departments. (Oxford did not follow suit until

1959.) It occupied the north wing of the former Anatomy School, on the New Museums site in the centre of the town, and boasted a distinctive green door (which was rescued by nostalgic former Maths Lab users when the service moved to a far grander Computer Laboratory in 1969).

The Director of the Maths Lab was Dr Maurice Wilkes, who had been appointed before the war but was almost immediately diverted to war work. Wilkes had been a radio enthusiast since boyhood. He had bought his first valve for the substantial sum of 12s 6d (62½p, equivalent to half a week's pay for a junior clerk in the 1920s). His ability as an undergraduate and then a graduate student working with calculating devices had won him notice from his academic superiors, and he was the obvious choice to take care of the day-to-day running of the Mathematical Laboratory when it was established in 1937. His brief was 'to advance knowledge of the science of mathematical computation, to promote and direct research in it, and to supervise the work of the Laboratory'. But war intervened before he had done much more than equip the lab with some desk calculating machines. He was posted to work on the electronics of radar at the government Telecommunications Research Establishment in Great Malvern.

After this wartime experience of electronics, Wilkes returned to Cambridge with much more ambitious ideas. Writing to Goldstine in January 1946, Hartree noted that Wilkes had asked about progress in the United States on electronic computers. Hartree must have given a satisfactory response, because the following month Wilkes wrote to the university authorities, arguing that they should venture into electronic computing. 'I think Cambridge should take its part,' he asserted in a statement with echoes of David's challenge to Goliath, 'in trying to catch up some of the lead the Americans have in this subject.' His memorandum optimistically suggested that a single research student or research assistant should be taken on for this purpose, prompting Hartree (who had not yet taken up his Cambridge post, but had clearly seen Wilkes's memo) gently to point out to the younger man the enormous scale of the ENIAC enterprise.

The exchange of information between Philadelphia and Cambridge continued. In May 1946 another British visitor to ENIAC, Dr Leslie J. Comrie of the Scientific Computing Service in London, returned with one of the twenty-six copies of von Neumann's 'A First Draft of a Report on the EDVAC', which had been given to him by Goldstine. Despite his status as an officer in the US Army, Goldstine's instincts were always academic rather than military and he wanted to see the Moore School work appreciated as widely as possible. He effectively saw to it that security restrictions on documents related to ENIAC and EDVAC were lifted as soon as possible after the war, and circulated von Neumann's paper generously to those he regarded as comrades in the electronic computing enterprise. This willingess to use wartime developments to peacetime advantage was in complete contrast to British government attitudes to its own secret computer project, Colossus. While visiting Cambridge, Comrie lent his copy of the report to Wilkes overnight, and the young mathematician sat up until the small hours reading it with close attention. From that point on, he realised where the future lay. 'I recognised this at once as the real thing,' he said later, 'and from that time on never had any doubt as to the way computer development would go.'

In 1946, Wilkes received a last-minute invitation to attend a summer course on computing at the Moore School, a chance for the engineers who built ENIAC to show it off to an international audience. He almost did not make it. The seminar began on 8 July. Wilkes could not get a boat until 3 August, and even then it was a cargo boat, the *Drakensberg Castle*, with accommodation for twelve passengers but carrying thirty-five. (Only men were allowed on board, and along with the other passengers, Wilkes had to undergo a medical examination to make sure he qualified.) He finally arrived on 15 August, with only two weeks of the seminar left to run. But they were worth waiting for, and he also took the opportunity to meet Herman Goldstine, who filled him on what he had missed, and to talk informally to John Mauchly.

By the time he left, Wilkes felt he knew all there was to know about how to build an EDVAC-type computer. Sailing home on the *Queen Mary,* he began to draw up plans to build one for the Cambridge laboratory. That autumn he began to build and test the various units that would form the computer's basic elements. He needed no one's permission to do this; the atmosphere in the post-war universities was one of new beginnings, of re-establishing peacetime values, such as support for intellectual enquiry. On the scale at which he began the work, with no more than a couple of assistants, the university would simply pay the bills. To his delight, Wilkes was offered thousands of valves free from government surplus stores, by an official in the Ministry of Supply who seemed equally delighted to have disposed of them with so little trouble.

The first problem that he tackled in earnest was how to store programs and data. While the concept of the stored-program computer had been in circulation certainly since von Neumann joined the ENIAC team, and in a more abstract sense since the publication of Turing's 'On Computable Numbers', no one had yet built a working prototype. The so-called 'electronic brain', ENIAC, had a memory worse than the average goldfish. With its 18,000 valves, it could store no more than twenty ten-digit decimal numbers at a time (using 500 valves for each). Moreover, it was programmed by physically plugging up the necessary circuits with a spaghetti of patch leads; each time you wanted to run a new program, you had to unplug them all and start again. ENIAC might have been able to carry out 5,000 additions a second, but without greatly increased storage its usefulness would always be limited to applications similar to the ballistics calculations for which it was designed.

One possible approach to the memory problem was to keep the stored numbers circulating as trains of pulses until required. It was Presper Eckert, chief design engineer of ENIAC, who first proposed a way to do this, although he arrived too late at his solution to implement it in his first computer. Sound travels through liquids very much more slowly than electricity passes through wires. Pulses of electricity can be converted into pulses of sound by causing a quartz crystal to vibrate. Eckert realised that a train of electrical pulses could be converted into an ultrasound signal and transmitted much more slowly through a tube of mercury. When the pulse train reached the end of the tube it could be converted back into an electrical signal and then recycled through the tube as many times as required. A single, five-foot long tube could hold more than thirty numbers at a time in this way, making mercury delay line storage massively more efficient than the valve storage used on ENIAC.

After his visit to the Moore School in 1946, Wilkes was as well informed as anyone both about the logical design for a computer encapsulated in von Neumann's 'First Draft', and about the practical engineering solutions proposed by Eckert. He decided to build his machine with mercury delay line storage, but was faced with the difficult task of drawing up the design specifications from scratch. On his return to Cambridge, as he put it in his memoirs, 'fate dealt him the final ace' in the excellent hand he already held. By chance he ran into a former acquaintance, Tommy Gold (who later achieved distinction as one of the proponents, with Fred Hoyle and Hermann Bondi, of the steady-state theory of the origin of the Universe). Gold had worked on ultrasonic delay units for the reception of radar signals during the war. The delayed radar pulse would be combined with the following pulse to cancel out echoes from stationary objects such as hills and trees. Echoes from moving objects, such as ships or aeroplanes, would be different and therefore would not cancel out. This application of ultrasonic delay lines was well established before anyone thought of using them to store information in computers.

Gold sat down and gave Wilkes precise design specifications for the tubes that he would have to make for his mercury delay

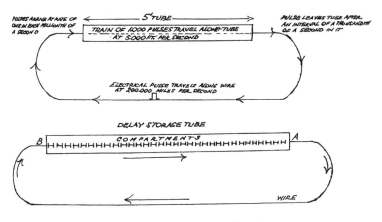

Diagrams illustrating the mercury delay line memory
circuits of EDSAC.

storage. His assistance saved the Cambridge team valuable time
that they would otherwise have had to spend finding the best
dimensions by trial and error. Looking at a mercury delay line
today – one was on display at the celebration of the Cambridge
computer's fiftieth anniversary in 1999 – it seems scarcely credible
that it could be part of a computer. To the untutored eye it looks
very much as if it ought to belong to a previous era of heavy
engineering. But heavy or not, it had to be a miracle of precision.
Working back from the number of pulses he wanted to keep in
circulation, Wilkes calculated that each line, or tube, had to be
exactly 5 feet 4 inches long, precise to one thousandth of an inch.
The internal diameter was exactly 1 inch. The steel tubes each held
half a ton of mercury. After several attempts, Wilkes finally had a
memory circuit running satisfactorily by February 1947.

The information in the circulating train of pulses was divided
among thirty-two 'compartments'. Each compartment could
contain an order or number in the form of a seventeen-binary-
digit 'word'. Each compartment had an 'address', defining which
of a battery of tubes it was in, and its position in the train of

compartments for that tube. The computer could gain access to data in the store once on each cycle through the tube. Because the use of this form of memory storage was so novel at the time, Wilkes called his computer the Electronic Delay Storage Automatic Calculator – EDSAC.

Lyons Goes to Cambridge

When Thompson and Standingford returned from their trip to the United States in June 1947, they found waiting for them a friendly letter from Douglas Hartree, inviting them to visit him and Maurice Wilkes at the Mathematical Laboratory to see how their computer was getting on. They arranged a visit for the following month. The Lyons men reported that they found Hartree and Wilkes 'keenly interested in our proposals for a commercial machine and prepared to make their knowledge and advice available. They had not previously realised the commercial possibilities of the machine, being preoccupied with its use in scientific research.'

Fresh from their tour of computer labs in the United States, Thompson and Standingford were extremely impressed with the progress Wilkes had made in less than a year. In fact, so far as they could judge, he was 'far in advance of the Moore School' in his work on the problem of memory. EDSAC was still twelve to eighteen months from completion, by Wilkes's estimate, but the memory units he had designed were working better than anything Thompson and Standingford had seen in the United States. They felt it necessary to warn Wilkes, however, that given the greater level of investment by the American designers, and especially the determination of Eckert and Mauchly to build a commercial machine, there might be machines on sale in the United States before he had finished if he did not get a move on.

Wilkes gave them to understand that it was only lack of funds that hampered his progress: with more money, and hence more people, he could implement his plans much more quickly. Being businessmen, they asked him how much. He said £2,000, adding that the Cambridge lab would be only too happy to help Lyons by running clerical jobs on EDSAC when it was ready, and by giving guidance on how to write programs.

Thompson and Standingford returned to Cadby Hall and put the finishing touches to the report on their United States visit, including a section on their meeting with Wilkes and Hartree in Cambridge. They followed this by setting out what they saw as the monumental opportunity facing Lyons. No one else in Britain, they emphasised, had realised the 'far reaching possibilities of electronic machines', which, they suggested, could offer a way out of the country's dire economic state. The company had a variety of options. It could just wait on the sidelines until a viable commercial machine became available, almost certainly in the United States. There would be no guarantee, however, that such a machine would be suitable for the kind of work Lyons needed. Alternatively, Lyons could take a more active role.

The report's authors listed the possibilities. Lyons could work closely with the Cambridge team, steering them towards the kind of machine that would suit their purposes, and offering them financial support; it could try to interest a large electrical firm such as GEC or EMI in taking on a commercially oriented project; it could work with and support Eckert and Mauchly in developing a commercial machine in the United States; it could appeal to the government to 'make all resources available to make Britain first in the field'; or it could build its own machine.

One of the first to see the draft report was John Simmons. Skimming the early sections, he turned quickly to Section D: 'Electronic Machines', and read it with a sense of mounting excitement. Here, it seemed, was a description of the machine he had dreamed about for almost twenty years. Somehow, he told Thompson, the company must be persuaded to take it on. He began his campaign with a letter to the venerable company secretary George Booth, who also had a copy of the report, urging him to look at the section on electronic machines. 'By the time I had finished it,' wrote Simmons, 'I found myself sharing the excitement which I know [Thompson and Standingford] possess. I feel with them that we are on the threshold of an extremely important development, in clerical work certainly but, very probably, in other fields as well, and that the company could, if it so desired, take a leading part.' Simmons added that he should like to send the report to the chairman, Harry Salmon, known as Mr Harry, with the recommendation that the board think about 'whether they are prepared to help to promote development in the field of electronic devices'.

Booth's reply was somewhat deflating. He had, he said, already read the electronic part of the report, and was annoyed by the authors' use of words such as 'memory' in the context of a machine. Unaware that the biological metaphor had been introduced into computer terminology by the great mathematician John von Neumann himself, he requested that all such 'journalese' be expunged before the report found its way to the boardroom. He warned Simmons against getting 'too excited', and thought the board would be reluctant to spend any money under the prevailing economic circumstances. But he conceded that the machine was 'most interesting, and should turn out to be of great value'. It was all the encouragement Simmons needed to write a memorandum to accompany the report when it was finally submitted to the board on 20 October 1947:

We believe that [Thompson and Standingford] have been able to get a glimpse of a development which will, in a few years' time, have a profound effect on the way clerical work (at least) is performed. Here, for the first time there is a possibility of a machine which will be able to cope, at almost incredible speed, with any variation of clerical procedure . . . What effect such a machine could have on the semi-repetitive work of the office needs only the slightest effort of imagination.

He enlarged upon the options for action listed by the report's authors, including an estimate of the costs of building a computer (£100,000) and an evaluation of the savings in day-to-day clerical costs it might make possible (£50,000 per year). He argued that unless business users were involved from the beginning, the benefits of such machines would be 'unnecessarily postponed for many years'.

Thinking through the various courses suggested by Thompson and Standingford, Simmons had in his own mind ruled out the first four. The Cambridge team was technically excellent, but would not really be interested in adapting their computer for use in an office, which had very different requirements. From what he knew of the electrical and office machine companies in the United Kingdom – and he knew them intimately – they had not even begun to think about electronic calculating machines. He had little faith in the post-war government's ability to initiate anything, whichever party was in power. The difficulty of obtaining dollars meant that buying an American machine was a non-starter, even if Eckert and Mauchly managed to get one built. That left only one option: Lyons must build its own machine.

The board considered the report on 20 October. Three days later the Lyons chairman Harry Salmon told Simmons informally that he was prepared to recommend a donation of £2,000–£3,000 to the Cambridge laboratory, with no strings attached. Furthermore, if and when the Cambridge machine had been shown to work, he would spend a further £50,000–£60,000 on building a machine for Lyons if it could be shown to make corresponding savings in clerical bills. (At 2002 prices, these sums would have been worth more than twenty times as much.) He felt that a second machine would almost certainly be necessary as a back-up in case of breakdowns, and did not expect the project to be showing such savings until the second machine was in operation. Even Simmons was astonished that his visionary, but expensive and risky proposal was so easily accepted. It was, he told an interviewer

towards the end of his life, a most extraordinary and very coura-
geous decision.

The formally dressed delegation from Lyons that walked into
the Mathematical Laboratory in Cambridge on 11 November 1947
was extremely impressive. It was led by the company secretary,
George Booth, then nearly eighty years old, accompanied by a
second Lyons 'employé director', Harold Bennett. Also in the
party were John Simmons, Raymond Thompson and Oliver Standingford. Cambridge in its turn fielded Douglas Hartree, Professor
of Mathematical Physics, and Dr Maurice Wilkes, newly appointed
director of the Maths Lab. Wilkes eagerly gave the visitors a tour of
the racks of valves and wires that represented the embryonic computer he was building. Then they got down to the business of the
meeting – a proposal that Cambridge might advise Lyons on building its own version of the same machine, in return for investment
in the Cambridge lab.

It was a highly amicable discussion. Simmons was immediately
impressed by the practical approach of the academics and pleased
to find that they were so willing to cooperate with others, 'even
laymen like ourselves'. Wilkes, for his part, knew Lyons to be a
go-ahead firm and was well aware that two of his visitors were
top-class Cambridge mathematics graduates. Booth finally came
to the point. He offered Wilkes £3,000 (about £60,000 in today's
money) and the services of an electrical engineer seconded from
Lyons. The only condition was that if the computer worked successfully, Lyons should be allowed to build a copy of it for its own
use. Wilkes accepted at once, and the parties shook hands warmly,
each convinced of the value of the collaboration.

The cheque arrived a few days later. Equally useful to Wilkes
was the electrical assistant Lyons chose to second to the Mathematical Laboratory. His name was Ernest Lenaerts, although he
was generally known as Len. From boyhood Lenaerts had been
fascinated by finding out how things worked, driving his parents to
distraction by taking things to pieces and reassembling them.

Leaving school at sixteen without any idea how to turn this natural technical ability into a career, he joined Lyons as a clerk in the Stock Department in the early 1930s. Realising that there must be something better, he studied assiduously at evening classes and applied to work in the Lyons chemical laboratories as a technician, but was not successful. It was the war that finally gave him the opportunity he was looking for. He joined the Royal Air Force and trained as a radio mechanic, working in radio countermeasures. Later he became responsible for operating the BBC transmitters at Alexandra Palace in North London, which the RAF used to jam enemy signals. He took the opportunity offered by the fixed posting to take a college course in electronics at the same time.

After the war he returned to Lyons, but persuaded the company to give him the post of radio mechanic rather than sending him back to a clerical job. At last he was allowed to give rein to his inventiveness. One of his projects was for a coin-operated dispensing machine, incorporating a microwave oven that would deliver hot sausages; he built a prototype and demonstrated it to the Lyons board. Lenaerts, it appeared to Thompson, who had been his boss in his days as a clerk, was just the person he was looking for: he knew about clerical work but he also had skills in electrical and electronic engineering, and was of an inventive turn of mind. His war service had given him the maturity and authority to cope with the challenge of working on a highly experimental project in the unfamiliar surroundings of a university laboratory.

Lenaerts was only too happy to accept the proposal. He started in Cambridge at the beginning of December 1947. 'We plunged him right into it,' says Wilkes, putting him to work on wiring the chassis that would hold the assembly of valves. By the time Lenaerts arrived, or shortly afterwards, the team in the Mathematical Laboratory had greatly expanded from the little group Thompson and Standingford had found on their first visit in the summer. There were three additional scientific staff, two of whom, like Wilkes, had wartime experience in radar research. And there were four additional engineers: one, an instrument maker, two ex-RAF and a boy trainee. In the first of a series of letters Lenaerts sent back to Lyons detailing the progress of the project, he wrote to Simmons that 'after a week at Cambridge I find that I have settled down to work quite comfortably with a very fine team of men'. He stayed until October the following year, acquiring invaluable practical expertise in the computer technology of the day.

Wilkes designed the machine himself. Not having a large engineering staff, he contracted out most of the wiring of the electronic units to a small firm in Cambridge, and his own team would then gradually assemble and test the complete computer. Although its performance was much more versatile, the EDSAC was modest in scale compared with the ENIAC, with just 3,000 valves. Nevertheless it was a substantial piece of engineering, that occupied most of a large room. Its electronic units were housed in racks that dwarfed its designers. They were lined up side by side with a wiring nightmare around the back. It eventually incorporated a battery of 32 mercury delay lines, encased in wooden coffers. This provided a total memory of 1,024 'words' – numbers or instructions – each consisting of 17 bits (the zeroes and ones of binary code). In modern terminology, that represents a little over 2 kilobytes (a byte consisting of 8 bits and a kilobyte, 1,024 bytes). No self-respecting PC currently on the market comes with less than 32,000 times as much in random access memory, before you even start talking about the capacity of the hard disk. But in the late 1940s, 1,024 words seemed enough for the kind of mathematical work Wilkes had in mind.

The First Programs

David Wheeler was one of two undergraduate volunteers who contributed to the early assembly work on EDSAC in 1946. The following year he started a PhD as one of Wilkes's first research students. The subject of his PhD was the programming of an electronic computer, the first thesis ever written on the subject. Wilkes had absorbed from his visit to the Moore School the idea that a computer could store its program as well as its data. But no one had previously given much thought to the practical question of formulating the set of instructions that comprised the program and communicating these instructions to the computer in a way that it could understand.

The limits of EDSAC's cognitive capabilities were set out with stark simplicity in a booklet prepared by Lyons staff in 1949, called *A Non-Technical Description of EDSAC: How the Cambridge Computer Works*: 'The construction of the machine is such that at any one time it cannot do more than add 1 and 1 together.' Far from being a machine that could think, EDSAC was a machine that could add binary 1 and binary 1 and make binary 10 – and that was all. Any calculation therefore had to be represented in the computer as a series of binary addition sums. The computer could then operate according to a set of conditional rules – its logic. Beginning from the rightmost digits and working leftwards, the rules are:

if both digits are 0, put 0 in the subtotal;
if one digit is 0 and one is 1, put 1 in the subtotal;
if both digits are 1, put 0 in the subtotal and carry 1 to the next column, to be added to the subtotal at a later stage. For example:

$$
\begin{array}{rr}
 & 11011011 \\
+ & 10001010 0 \\
\hline
= & 101100101 1 \\
\end{array}
$$

It was essential that programmers kept in mind the workings of the machine. Each addition was carried out by the part of the computer called the arithmetic unit, although somewhat confusingly it was also known as the computor (as distinct from the store,

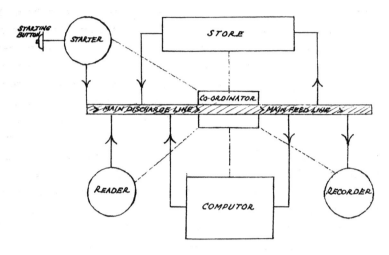

Diagram of the main components of the Cambridge computer, from
the Lyons document, *A Non-Technical Description of EDSAC.*

control unit and input and output units). The total would be held
in the part of the arithmetic unit called the accumulator, rather
as the display on a pocket calculator records the current total.
But unless the next step in the program involved adding to that
total, the computer had to be instructed to send it to a designated
storage compartment until it was needed again.

Programmers had to be constantly aware of the capacity of
each of the memory units, if necessary shuffling data or instructions from one to another as the calculation proceeded. This need
for at least a working knowledge of hardware is long since a thing
of the past for most computer users. 'It's like driving,' says David
Wheeler. 'You don't have to know how the engine works any more
to drive a car. You used to have to know where carburettors were
because you might have to clean them.'

Wheeler devised an approach to programming the EDSAC
that was soon widely copied. His thesis formed the basis of the
world's first textbook on programming, *The Preparation of Programs*

for an Electronic Digital Computer by Maurice Wilkes, David Wheeler and Stanley Gill (1951). Despite its British authorship, the book was published in the United States by Addison-Wesley Press, and so has American spelling; perhaps it was for this reason that the English spelling of 'programme', in the particular case of computer programs, gradually died out in the United Kingdom during the 1950s.

The immediate problem in writing a program is that humans and computers do not speak the same language. Computers think in binary code. Humans can learn binary code, and can become quite good at writing instructions in it; but it is extraordinarily cumbersome and a tired programmer can easily make expensive mistakes. To avoid this problem, Wheeler and his colleagues devised a simple code, called the order code, that was economical and easy for humans to write and remember, but also straightforward for the computer to convert into binary.

The code consisted of the 26 letters of the alphabet, plus four more punctuation characters giving a total of 30 different instructions, and decimal numbers denoting the addresses of the locations in the store where the data was held. The overriding consideration, says David Wheeler, was that the system would be easy for programmers to use. 'We chose the letters to represent particular instructions – we could choose more or less at will,' he says. 'There were some natural choices: A was chosen for add, S for subtract, T for transfer and so on.' If a programmer wanted to instruct the computer to 'add the content of location 58 into the accumulator', for example, all he or she had to write down was 'A58'.

Having developed the order code in which programs were to be written, the team's next task was to find a way to install the programs into the memory of the machine. Ever on the lookout for tried and tested existing technologies that could be incorporated into his project, Wilkes followed the lead of other computer pioneers in settling on punched paper tape. A key punch operator would type the program on a keyboard similar to a typewriter keyboard, except that instead of letters on paper, the machine punched holes in tape according to a five-position code. The tape was then fed into a tape reader, which converted the code into electrical pulses and transmitted it to the computer.

The Cambridge team used a five-hole code to represent the letters of the alphabet, and the numerals from o to 9 were simply punched in the appropriate binary code. This gave them a system for delivering any combination of numbers and instructions to the computer in the form of electrical impulses. But before the computer could be made to work, it had to know what to do with these instructions. That required another program to tell the computer how to read any subsequent programs. Wilkes and his colleagues avoided what might have appeared as a nightmare of infinite regress by hard-wiring the computer's first set of instructions, called 'initial orders', into the machine. When the operator loaded a programme he inserted a tape in the tape reader and pressed the 'start' button that would activate a set of switches and place the first thirty-one instructions into the memory of the machine (later the number was increased to forty). These instructions included one to read the program tape and install it in the computer's memory. The initial orders also carried out the conversion from decimal to binary numbers, so that programmers did not need to worry about thinking in binary or including a conversion step in their programs.

On 6 May 1949, without any fanfare, the EDSAC successfully ran its first program, computing and printing out the squares of all the numbers from o to 99. The entry in the daily log laconically recorded 'May 6. Machine in operation for first time. Printed table of squares (o–99), time for program 2 mins. 35 sec. Four tanks [delay lines] of battery 1 in operation.' David Wheeler was rather proud of the table of squares, not so much from the point of view of the arithmetic part of it, but that the machine printed it out in decimal digits. 'Almost every other machine started with a table of squares,' he says, 'except they printed them out in binary ...

There's a lot of difference in the programming – to do a table of squares the only complicated thing is the printing.'

From the point of view of people who actually wanted to use a computer rather than demonstrate its principles, EDSAC's chattering into life was one of the most important milestones in the development of modern computers. By modern standards it was hardly user-friendly, but it was certainly usable by anyone who could master the business of writing a program and punching it out on tape. It took in its programs and data automatically through a punched tape reader, and output its results directly to a printer. In the years that followed, the Maths Lab held open house for a constant stream of chemists, astronomers, physicists and mathematicians all eager to write their own programs and make use of the machine's powers of calculation. But strictly speaking EDSAC was not the first stored program computer in operation. That honour went the previous year to a tiny experimental machine built in Manchester.

The mercury delay line was not the only option open to early computer builders as a memory device. Although it was the preferred choice of Eckert and Mauchly, elsewhere in the United States the research laboratories of RCA, which had been taken over by the army during the war, had come up with a device called the Selectron that was based on a cathode ray tube – the same technology used in television screens and computer monitors. When electrons hit the screen of a cathode ray tube, they trigger a flash of phosphorescence that decays only slowly. Like the mercury delay line, the Selectron had been used to cancel out radar echoes from static objects. Visiting the United States after the war, the British radar engineer F. C. Williams of the Telecommunications Research Establishment conceived the idea of developing the Selectron as the basis of a stored program computer.

Shortly afterwards Williams was appointed to the Chair in Electrical Engineering at Manchester University and he took the project with him together with a research colleague, Tom Kilburn. The aim of the project was to hold information on the screen by constantly refreshing the display before it faded. As with the mercury delay lines, this would keep the same information cycling until something happened to change it.

Williams and Kilburn built the first Manchester University computer initially to test the tube as a means of storing digital information. A secondary consideration was that it might provide valuable experience that could be put to use in building a full-scale machine. The 'Baby' machine, as it was nicknamed, could store only thirty-two words, had very limited arithmetical capabilities (it could only subtract), and no means at all of installing programs and data automatically or printing results. Operators had to add numbers and instructions to the store, in binary code, by laboriously pushing buttons, and read the results off the screen. But on 21 June 1948 it successfully ran a program and thereby gained the accolade of being the world's first stored program computer to come into operation.

By the following year the Manchester engineers had produced the Manchester Mark 1 (also known as MADM or the Manchester Automatic Digital Machine), an expansion of the original prototype with more storage and other original architectural features. At this point the British government, which had shown no interest at all in EDSAC, began to wake up to what was going on. Sir Ben Lockspeiser, then government chief scientist, was so impressed by MADM that he gave the defence electronics firm Ferranti Ltd, through the Ministry of Supply, a contract for £175,000 to build a fully engineered computer based on the same technology. The Ferranti Mark 1 was installed at Manchester University in 1951, neck and neck with Eckert and Mauchly's UNIVAC as the first electronic computer to be delivered by a commercial manufacturer.

The Manchester work had a number of significant implications for the future development of computing. The Williams Tube (as it became known, although recently historians have attempted to redress the balance in favour of Tom Kilburn, who shared most of the patents, by calling it the Williams-Kilburn Tube) was later licensed to a number of American computer manufacturers, including IBM. It inspired the first government investment in computing in the United Kingdom. And it launched for the first time in the United Kingdom the idea that computers might be built commercially for sale, rather than constructed as research projects in universities.

Between them the Cambridge and Manchester teams demonstrated that when it came to practical competence in electronic engineering design, construction and operation, British computer scientists were second to none. 'The first modern electronic computers, by any definition, were built in Britain,' wrote the American historian Kenneth Flamm of the Brookings Institution in 1988. Another historian, John Hendry, agrees that 'In the late 1940s Britain shared with America world leadership in the exciting new technology of computers.' It might seem remarkable that poorly funded British researchers should steal a march on the various American groups who were working on computers at the time. After all, the Americans had access to generous amounts of government (mostly defence) cash, they had the experience of building ENIAC, and they had made all the necessary theoretical advances in the 'First Draft of a Report on the EDVAC'.

Maurice Wilkes has a simple explanation. 'Our object was very different from Eckert and Mauchly,' he says. 'They set out to build a computer to the highest standards, which they could sell. Whereas we wanted to make a machine that would work sufficiently.' It seemed that in the United States, the best had been the enemy of the good. Wilkes, in contrast, worked according to the philosophy that had governed the radar research in which he participated at TRE during the war. 'In the war you learned how to do things, and you learned how to do things quickly,' he says. 'We had the term "crash program". A squadron of aircraft had to be equipped with a radar device by such and such a date, and a crash program took place. Instruments were made by hand and installed. [The EDSAC project] was a crash program, even though it took a few years rather than a few weeks. People worked hard, but it wasn't a forced march – it was just the way the thing was directed. Corners were cut judiciously. It was a definite policy of mine that if something had been made to work – a particular chassis had been made to do its job, for example – then that was that. You didn't try and find a more elegant way of doing it or one which involved less equipment, you just accepted it. It was a matter of not getting interested in sidelines, keeping your nose to the grindstone.'

In 1950 EDSAC began to provide a service to university users, and continued for eight years until superseded by its successor, EDSAC 2. Among the first users were Douglas Hartree, for numerical analysis; the X-ray crystallographer John Kendrew, who won a Nobel prize for solving the structure of the protein myoglobin in 1962; and the astronomer Martin Ryle and his colleagues for analysing data from the new Cambridge radio telescope. In subsequent decades the Mathematical Laboratory continued to set the standard for computer services in British universities, becoming the first to develop a system that gave multiple users access to a central computer and going on to pioneer a network of connected machines called the Cambridge Ring. It also presided over groundbreaking research in subjects such as computer-aided design, and many of its staff and graduates are now in influential positions throughout the computer industry.

Among the first to hear the news of EDSAC's first successful operation was Simmons at Lyons. It was the green light he had been waiting for. If the Cambridge Mathematical Laboratory could build a computer that worked, then so could Lyons.

4

A Computer for Lyons

The chairman looked up as the clerk came apologetically into the boardroom to hand him a note. Gathered around the mahogany table were the Salmon and Gluckstein family board members, together with the longest-standing member of them all, company secretary George Booth. Their chairman Harry Salmon glanced quickly at the note. It was from John Simmons, and reported that the Cambridge engineers had telephoned that morning, 8 May 1949, to say that EDSAC had run its first successful programs. He was now, Mr Harry told his fellow board members, asking them to authorise the building of the Lyons computer. There was not much need for discussion: Mr Harry had given his word two years before that Lyons would fund the computer if the Cambridge experiment worked. The heads around the table nodded in assent; Mr Harry unscrewed the cap of his fountain pen, wrote on a piece of paper and passed it to the clerk. The clerk brought the note back to Simmons: it bore the single word, 'Yes'.

John Simmons had lost no time in preparing the ground at Lyons for the day when the company would build its own computer. Even before the moment Booth had shaken hands on the agreement with Wilkes, in Simmons's mind the project had already begun. He first addressed himself not to the engineering aspects of the enterprise, but to the subject he had developed into an art form at Lyons: analysing the requirements of each clerical job and planning how best to meet them. The only difference was that now it would be a computer doing the work, rather than a roomful of clerks.

The first task was to identify the jobs that the computer could do, to establish that it would be cost-effective to automate them, and to specify how they should be done. Simmons, who as comptroller at Lyons had too many responsibilities to do the work himself, thought it important enough to put someone on to it full time. Diverting a manager as senior as Raymond Thompson at this early stage would not have gone down well with the board. The obvious place to look for the requisite talent was in the department Simmons had created to solve Lyons's clerical problems, the Systems Research office. After the war, the day-to-day running of Systems Research was in the hands of another former management trainee of the 1930s, David Caminer.

Caminer was to play a key role in turning an essentially limited piece of technology into an elegant tool with a range of applications more ambitious than Simmons had ever dreamed possible. He has chronicled LEO's pioneering years himself, and remains today a trenchant observer of the computer scene. His history has turned out very differently from the future he imagined for himself as a rebellious schoolboy. Pugnacious and black-browed, the young David Caminer of the Depression-hit 1930s had been a left-wing idealist, burning with revolutionary fervour but with no real direction. His parents' pleas that he might study or earn a living fell on deaf ears. 'I had a weird idea,' he says, 'that all the old institutions – the law, the judiciary, the universities – were irrelevant in this age of unemployment and hunger marches – the new order was going to come and make things better than they were at the moment, so I really didn't give my attention to them at all.'

Almost as an afterthought he applied to Cambridge, though his school career had been less than diligent. 'I went up to Peterhouse for a scholarship,' he says, 'and I was enchanted by the scene in hall. And I thought this is very nice, I wish I'd done more work. Most my reading for this scholarship was done on the train going up to Cambridge. So they would have been very misguided on the

basis of the proficiencies I was able to offer to give me anything.'
They did not.

In desperation, his parents turned for advice to their next-door
neighbour, 'a very respectable gentleman who went off each morning in his wing collar, black jacket and striped trousers', who was
the manager of Retail Rounds at Lyons. He secured an interview
for their son with John Simmons, on the strength of which
Caminer was hired in 1936 to work as a management trainee in
Management Accounts. From the first he was hooked, thriving on
the intellectual challenge of Simmons's drive to improve the
efficiency of the organisation. But after only three years, like so
many, his career at Lyons was interrupted by the war. While many
of the British computer pioneers spent their war years as boffins
and backroom boys, contributing to vital developments such as
radar and code-breaking, Caminer joined an infantry regiment, the
Green Howards, and went off to fight in North Africa with the
8th Army. In March 1943 he was seriously wounded during an
attack in Tunisia and lost a leg.

Returning to Lyons on his recovery in 1944, Caminer took over
Systems Research, carrying on the task that Simmons had begun a
decade or more before. 'There were quite a lot of things to tidy up,'
he says 'but we had reached nearly the end of the road. The clerical
operation was already remarkably efficient, the showcase of the
world, and so we really did need something revolutionary.'

It was to Systems Research that Simmons turned in his search
for new recruits to his vision of the Lyons computer, who would
begin the process of designing clerical applications to run on it.
Caminer himself had too many responsibilities to devote his full
attention to the computer project, and in researching how to automate clerical jobs he had the assistance of one of his junior
colleagues, an ex-army wireless specialist called Derek Hemy.

Hemy had joined Lyons straight from school as a management trainee in 1939. 'I thought about university,' he said, 'but my
family was not well off and I thought I had better get out and earn

something. I started on the magnificent sum of 25 bob [£1.25] a week.' Barely had he learned the business when war broke out and he left to join the army. After two years of service as an ordinary soldier in the chemical warfare division of the Royal Engineers, he was selected to train as an officer in the Royal Corps of Signals. He was then sent on the officers' advanced wireless course 'because he knew a little calculus', and by 1943 he was in command of an outfit in Harrogate cryptically known as AR 13.

AR 13 was involved in intercepting enemy signals and developing a technique known as 'radio fingerprinting'. The idea was to print out traces of enemy signals on long rolls of photographic paper and to identify the transmitter that sent them from characteristic quirks in the signal frequencies. 'I don't know if we affected the war at all,' said Hemy, 'but we got some very good results, mainly because of my senior classifier Corporal Kirkwood. She was brilliant at it.' Margaret Kirkwood was the most senior of the mostly female staff of sixty at AR 13 and played a key role in the successful development of radio fingerprinting. Hemy admired her for more than her skill – as soon as the war was over they were married.

Back at Lyons in 1946 Hemy found that his status had soared. It was known that he had performed well on the advanced wireless course and done something secret with signals, and to his surprise he found a rumour in circulation that he had 'invented radar'. Despite Hemy's protestations that it was all down to knowing a little calculus, Lyons clearly felt that the plans they had had for him as a nineteen-year-old trainee were no longer suitable. They sent him to work in Systems Research.

Hemy went to his new post with some trepidation. Caminer had the reputation of being 'not a comfortable person to work for'. He did not suffer fools, and drove his staff relentlessly, although no more relentlessly than he drove himself. Hemy was not easily intimidated, however. After one early showdown, which ended with Hemy slamming the phone down on his irate superior, they developed a productive working relationship based on mutual respect. 'After that I didn't mind speaking my mind to him,' said Hemy, 'and he pulled no punches. But he accepted that if I agreed I was wrong I'd admit it, no flannel.' What Hemy learned from Caminer was invaluable when it came to designing systems for the computer. 'With Caminer running Systems Research, you didn't just look at office methods,' said Hemy. 'You tried to look at the requirements of the business. That was Caminer's biggest contribution to Lyons, this idea that whatever your system is, it has got to meet the needs of the people at the sharp end. If it didn't do that, elegance didn't matter.'

According to Hemy's recollection, on 30 September 1947 he was called into the office of assistant comptroller Geoffrey Mills and asked to begin work planning for the arrival of the computer. Simmons, he remembered, was beginning to drive the project forward three weeks before the Thompson and Standingford report had even been formally considered by the Board, and certainly before Lenaerts had begun his secondment at Cambridge. Hemy was to remain part of Systems Research but to work full time on the computer project. He found himself in a rather privileged position, in that other members of Systems Research had to complete their projects to rather tight budgets, while he was the first to be given an assignment with no limit in financial terms.

His task was to look at all the clerical jobs that might be done by the computer, calculate the volume of work involved and estimate the savings that might be made over doing the jobs manually. It was clear, however, that this task was only the preliminary to devising the programs that would be necessary to run the jobs on the machine. Accordingly, Thompson solemnly handed him the only document on programming he could find. This thick volume turned out to be the programming manual for the Harvard Mark I, an electromechanical automatic calculator built by IBM engineers and Howard Aiken of Harvard University during the Second World War. 'It meant nothing to me, and told me nothing,' says Hemy.

So after the first six months he followed Lenaerts to Cambridge, ostensibly to spend a fortnight learning about programming on the EDSAC. Wilkes was friendly and welcoming but told Hemy, 'I'm afraid you'll have to ferret around for yourself – we've been too busy to think about programming.' He then handed over a 'very thick and quite chaotic file of rough notes and memoranda', which Hemy spent the first week trying to puzzle his way through. But he had seen a computer for the first time, even if it was not working yet; and the opportunity to talk to Wilkes and his colleagues was invaluable. During the second week Hemy worked with Ben Noble, who with David Wheeler was developing the 'order code', the set of alphabetical and numeric characters in which programs for EDSAC were to be written. At least he could return to Lyons equipped with a language – even of just a few words – that would enable him to instruct a computer in its business.

By the summer of 1948 David Wheeler, then still a PhD student, had become the principal programmer on the EDSAC team. He spent part of his vacation that year working with Caminer and Hemy at Lyons, sharing his general programming expertise and learning about the special requirements of business computing. Wheeler found the novelty of thinking about commercial programs rather than mathematical ones rather enjoyable. The affable young graduate student and the two ex-army Lyons managers became mutually and happily absorbed in the intricacies of systems design and programming. The three of them began to put together the first pilot program of clerical work, which they hoped to test on EDSAC as soon as it was working.

They chose a section of the payroll, not because it was the job that would save the company the most money but because it had a number of characteristics that made it a good test of the computer's capabilities. It involved both data that did not change from one week to the next, such as each employee's name, National Insurance number, tax rate and rate of pay, and variable quantities such as hours worked and any bonuses due. It had to print out a payslip showing gross pay, deductions for tax and net pay. It had to calculate down to the last penny the number of coins of each denomination that would be needed to make up the pay packets of all the employees in the system. It had to carry forward totals for the tax year to date. And most importantly, it had to work reliably to a regular weekly deadline. This was almost certainly the first commercial program ever run on a computer. Unfortunately the first version never worked; delivered eventually by Hemy to Wheeler to run when there was a gap in EDSAC's busy schedule, it stopped after two minutes, with no indication of what had gone wrong. It was a valuable lesson, and thereafter Lyons's programs were written in shorter sections or stages, so that it was easier to locate faults when they occurred.

The initial investigations and ventures into programming quickly made it clear that the size of the program and the volume of data required for an application such as payroll would be beyond the capacity of EDSAC's memory. Any Lyons computer would need to have a store that was twice as large. David Caminer began a long-lasting battle with the mathematicians Simmons and Thompson to get them to realise how much greater the memory demands of a clerical system would be. 'Mathematical jobs were very simple,' he says. 'It was something Simmons never really understood – the mathematical jobs were simple whereas the clerical jobs were terribly complicated.'

One of the reasons the clerical jobs were complicated was that the same data had to be used over and over again for different purposes. Data preparation, which in practice meant young women punching away at cards or tape, was one of the most expensive parts of the process in terms of both time and money. If the computer did not use the data efficiently, then nothing would be saved over manual methods. 'We had to have integrated systems, we didn't just do the job for one department,' says Caminer. 'That data had to be used for every department that was affected. So for an item of sales in cakes the computer had not only to work out the value of those cakes and how much profit was going to be made on them, but also to make sure that the chap who bought the cakes paid up for them. And from the same data we had to know how many cakes the bakers were going to make, how much they were allowed to spend on ingredients, how much energy they would use. And the final step was to compare what they had actually spent with what they were supposed to spend, and to what extent the company was making the profit it had budgeted for. All that had to be built in. If the machine had storage capacity sufficient for all we wanted to put into it we could have done that without a great deal of worry. But of course it had negligible storage space. So how to use the storage space successively to accommodate all these things became a very nice problem, which I think we solved quite conclusively. We were able to do things with tiny stores that now take megabytes – gigabytes.'

Time for the Engineers

Well before EDSAC had fully proved its worth, the favourable reports Simmons was receiving from Lenaerts and Hemy indicated that it was only a matter of time until it was up and running. And when that time came, Lyons had to be ready to begin at once. In September 1948 Simmons persuaded Mr Harry that it was time that Lyons thought about engaging 'an expert for the building of our machine', even though the prototype, EDSAC, was not yet working. Accordingly he placed an advertisement in the scientific journal *Nature*; and within a few days he had an application on his desk from a Cambridge physicist, John Pinkerton.

Pinkerton was the son of a surgeon who was also an amateur radio enthusiast, and as a boy he proved equally captivated by his father's hobby. He built his first radio set by the age of twelve, and entered the University of Cambridge to read Natural Sciences in

1937. After graduating he was sent to join the team of radar researchers at the Telecommunications Research Establishment in Malvern, returning to Cambridge when the war ended to read for a PhD in ultrasonics.

When Douglas Hartree was appointed Plummer Professor of Mathematical Physics at Cambridge in 1946, he gave an inaugural lecture entitled 'Calculating Machines: Recent and Prospective Developments'. By this time Hartree had already been to the United States and seen ENIAC, and his talk was of the incredible speeds such machines could achieve, and the remarkable things they would be able to do. In his talk he emphasised the need to take a 'machine's eye view' of any problem so as not to be caught out by unforeseen events in the course of a program. Given his audience, it was perhaps not surprising that the second half of his lecture dwelt on applications of the computer in mathematical physics, together with an acknowledgement that it might also be useful in number theory and applied statistics. But another comment suggests that he saw the possibility of wider use. 'It may well be,' he concluded with what now seems like understatement, 'that the high speed digital computor (*sic*) will have as great an influence on civilisation as the advent of nuclear power.'

John Pinkerton was among those in the packed audience to hear these prophetic words, which set the Cambridge mathematical community buzzing. He was intrigued, and as word spread that Maurice Wilkes was building a computer for the Maths Lab, he took to dropping in there to hear the occasional talks Wilkes gave on the project's progress. Pinkerton and Wilkes had known each other for almost a decade, first as student members of the Cambridge University Wireless Society, and then during the war as radar researchers at TRE in Malvern. They continued to meet informally from time to time.

Some time during 1948, Wilkes happened to mention to Pinkerton that Lyons was planning to build its own machine, based on EDSAC. So when, later that year, Wilkes drew his attention to a cryptic advertisement in the pages of the science journal *Nature*, Pinkerton did not have too much difficulty in guessing who had placed it. The advertisement was for 'a graduate electronics engineer aged 25–35', but gave no details of the work proposed, nor of the employer. Applicants were asked to write to a box number. John Pinkerton sent off an application, and waited to see what would happen next.

At the time of his application to Lyons Pinkerton had just completed his PhD thesis at the Cavendish Laboratory on the absorption of ultrasonic waves in liquids. Although quiet and self-effacing, he was fired with intellectual curiosity and derived huge satisfaction from asking new questions and solving problems. He had assumed that he would follow an academic career, and had hoped to be appointed to a college fellowship in Cambridge; no fellowship had materialised, however. At the age of twenty-nine he was engaged to be married, and although his fiancée Helen was herself about to embark on a highly successful career in the Civil Service – she took up the post of private secretary to the radical Labour minister Edith Summerskill immediately after their marriage – he felt it was incumbent on him to get a proper job. The post of chief engineer on the Lyons computer project was the first that genuinely appealed to him.

Thompson sounded out Wilkes on what he thought of this man Pinkerton, and received a glowing reference in reply. In the middle of December 1948 Pinkerton was invited to Cadby Hall for an interview. He was extremely impressed; the interview was unlike anything he had experienced anywhere else. When Simmons and Thompson interviewed someone for a senior post, their whole effort was geared to giving him (it was invariably a he at this stage) as full a picture as possible of the company and the job, so that the candidate could assess how well he might fit in. Pinkerton's interview lasted from 10.00 in the morning until 5.30 in the afternoon. It included a working demonstration of the bakery sales invoicing system, using the Recordak microfilm that the Systems Research office had introduced before the war. He had 'a very nice lunch', and interviews with both Simmons and Thompson.

They explained that they wanted someone to build a version of EDSAC, which he and they both knew was not yet working. Pinkerton thought they were 'perhaps a little mad, but it was going to be great fun'. He was ushered in to meet the octogenarian company secretary George Booth, who asked, 'Young man, do you think you can make this machine work?' He replied with great honesty, 'Yes, but it may not be very reliable.' Pinkerton, always a realist and useful counterweight to the more idealistic Simmons and Thompson, knew that any machine with thousands of valves in it could never operate without a hitch.

For their part, Simmons and Thompson were entirely satisfied that the tall, bespectacled academic was the man they needed. The job was clearly Pinkerton's if he wanted it, and he decided that he did. A modest man to the end of his life, he remarked in an interview that five years working on electronic pulse circuitry for radar at TRE and three years on ultrasonics at Cambridge put him 'in as good a position as anyone else to become a computer engineer'. Today, Maurice Wilkes's considered opinion is that Pinkerton was 'the most able of all the industrial computing engineers at that time'. To many others he was simply a genius, combining a profound understanding of the theoretical background to electronics with a skilled pair of hands: he could tackle any practical problem, and loved to do so. His wife Helen could not recall any piece of domestic equipment ever leaving the house to be mended; David Caminer remembered Pinkerton blowing glass to make a device for filling the mercury tubes.

Most important of all, he was an effective team leader, setting high standards by example rather than exhortation, and deploying the talents of his laughably small staff where they could be most effective. He was to become one of four key Lyons staff – the others being Simmons, Thompson and Caminer – without whom the project might never have succeeded as it did. But whereas the other three were carrying forward a Lyons tradition of forward thinking and systems design, Pinkerton was to head a team of computer engineers for which there was really no precedent within the company – and scarcely anywhere else.

Pinkerton joined Lyons in January 1949. The following month, in the first of a series of reports on the development of LEO which he addressed to Booth, Simmons asked for the sum of £400 so that Pinkerton and Lenaerts could set up a workshop and begin the engineering work on the Lyons computer. They moved into 'two small rooms over a gatehouse' in a part of the Cadby Hall site known as St Mary's College, which had formerly been a Catholic seminary. There they began to experiment with electronic circuits built from second-hand components, while Pinkerton made a number of trips to Cambridge to learn all he could about building a computer.

In the context of a modern university, where departments feel compelled to maximise the potential for generating income from their inventions, such a relationship between an academic laboratory and a commercial company would be impossible. But Wilkes knew where his priorities lay. 'We made the place entirely open. You mustn't forget that there was much openness in those early days; I was very conscious of the extraordinary generosity of Eckert and Mauchly and the Moore School in sharing their expertise, not only with me but generally. In any case,' he adds, 'I hadn't got time to fool around with things like intellectual property agreements.'

After the historic board meeting in May 1949 that gave the computer project the final green light, work started in earnest on building the machine in a room on the second floor of WX block at Cadby Hall that Simmons had earmarked long before. Always a stickler for the exact use of language, Simmons insisted that the word 'computor' should be used only to refer to the arithmetic unit, the part of the machine that carried out calculations. The

LEO was constructed in the administrative block at Cadby Hall.

system as a whole, he suggested, was the Electronic Office. Three months later he noted in his diary that his pet project now had a name: 'It seems to be generally agreed that it would be appropriate to christen the electronic machine project LEO (Lyons Electronic Office).' LEO therefore became exceptional not only in being the first office computer but in being the first to break from the tradition of more-or-less meaningless acronyms (ENIAC, EDSAC, UNIVAC) and serial numbers (Harvard Mark I, Manchester Mark I, and a whole series of IBM model numbers). Was Simmons showing an unexpectedly whimsical side in adopting the name of a popular children's cartoon character, Leo the Lion? If so he never admitted it.

With the official launch and baptism of the LEO project, Simmons felt that its progress should be given greater priority among his other duties as chief comptroller. His reports to the board dropped increasingly heavy hints about the need, especially for himself and Thompson, to devote more time to LEO. He wrote in the summer of 1949:

It is no exaggeration to say, that the whole organisation of the work to be undertaken by the electronic office will need to be thought out afresh . . . We are engaged in planning nothing less than a revolution in the mass clerical operations of the Company and, if it is to be accomplished successfully, it is clear that it will need a thorough revolution of all our preconceived notions of clerical technique and organisation.

By the following March, he was writing to Booth that Thompson, who was still officially chief assistant comptroller, while simultaneously heading the LEO project, was trying to do too much, and that, 'One day [he] should be relieved of his other responsibilities.' He added quickly, 'I am conceited enough to think that I can contribute something, Thompson needs someone to consult with.' He proposed a full-time management structure for LEO, with Thompson at its head, Pinkerton in charge of the technical side, Caminer in charge of programming and Oliver Standingford supervising the flow of work from departments to the computer. Booth (and hence the board) accepted his proposals in principle, vetoing only the transfer of Oliver Standingford from his post as assistant comptroller.

Despite Standingford's key role in placing an electronic computer firmly on Lyons's agenda – he liked to think of himself as 'the father of the idea' – he was to play no further part in its development, much to his regret. The board clearly decided that the project did not need two managers at such a senior level, and as Thompson was the mathematician, it was Thompson whom they saw as most appropriate. Soon afterwards Standingford left Cadby Hall and became a manager with Walkers Dairies in Liverpool, which made Lyons Maid ice cream. He remained for ever an evangelist for better office management, writing several textbooks, including one that accompanied a BBC TV series in 1972.

The LEO development team formally came together in May 1950, with Caminer and Hemy moving from Systems Research to join Pinkerton and the engineers in WX Block, the building where the computer was being constructed, and Thompson taking overall charge. The transfer to work on something that was essentially a tool rather than an arm of the whole Lyons business seemed suspiciously like a demotion at first to Caminer, who at the time would have preferred to stay in Systems Research: 'We wanted to carry on with the whole, rather than have it split off,' he says. But it took very little time before the demands of designing and programming the new machine became all-absorbing.

At about the same time Thompson put the word around Lyons that he was interested in recruiting bright trainees as programmers. This produced Leo Fantl from the Labour Planning Office (where his tasks had included time-and-motion studies of office cleaning, carried out by the trainees themselves in the small hours of the morning so as not to alarm the cleaners), John Grover from Bakery Sales, and Anthony Barnes from the Statistical Office.

According to Fantl, they were not formally tested for the job. He had an interview with Thompson in which Thompson did all the talking, and a few weeks later he was transferred. Fantl had arrived in Britain from Czechoslovakia in 1939 as a fifteen-year-old refugee, joining the RAF as soon as he was old enough. All the mathematics he knew he had learned either during his technical training in the air force or from correspondence courses. The round face behind his glasses was always cheerful and good humoured. Grover was also ex-RAF, having previously been an apprentice engineer; quiet and methodical, he could always be relied on to follow instructions to the letter. Barnes was a Cambridge graduate in engineering, bright but occasionally undisciplined. All three turned out to have a natural aptitude for the task of programming – much to the delight of Derek Hemy, who had to train them. But in 1950 the computer was still not ready to run commercial programs, and much of their early effort was spent writing test programs designed to expose weaknesses undetected by the engineers.

Building LEO

The total time taken to build a modern PC probably amounts to a matter of minutes. Circuits are mass produced, etched in silicon or printed on boards. Even when several such boards are assembled in one box, together with hard and CD-Rom drives, there are just a few contacts to screw down. And the completed product, in the case of a laptop, is not much bigger than a large hardback book.

When Simmons began to plan for the building of the Lyons computer, soon after Pinkerton's arrival, he set aside 2,500 square feet of floor space on the second storey of WX Block at Cadby Hall. Even that was modest compared with the vast volume occupied by ENIAC. Computers in the late 1940s were big, expensive and time-consuming to build and to run. But essentially they consisted of exactly the same elements as a modern PC: an input device, a store or memory, a processing unit (combining control and arithmetic units) and an output device. The EDSAC team in Cambridge made all these elements by adapting pre-existing technology such as thermionic valves and paper tape readers: they did not have to invent anything.

When Pinkerton came to copy Wilkes's design, he made the pragmatic decision that he would make no alterations unless he understood why something was the way it was. 'To start with, since we didn't understand very well why it was designed the way it was,' he said in an interview later, 'we didn't make very many changes at all.' Pinkerton's goal was the same as Wilkes's had been: not to make the best possible computer but to make a computer that could quickly be put into use. This philosophy was shared by all those involved; Simmons himself, in one of his reports to the board, explained that, 'The electronic office, as we conceive it, is essentially a users' machine.'

The work Hemy had carried out with David Wheeler before Pinkerton's arrival had served a very useful function. The payroll program that they wrote, although it was never ultimately used, gave an idea of the size of program that would be required to run on the Lyons computer. And it took no time at all to persuade Pinkerton that EDSAC had too little storage for the job. The first decision he made to diverge from the EDSAC design was that there would have to be twice as much memory – 64 mercury delay lines, instead of 32. Building these was a job for precision toolmakers, not electrical engineers, and so having had the designs redrawn in the Lyons engineering drawing office, Pinkerton contracted out the work of making the tubes to a manufacturer in the Midlands, the Coventry Gauge and Tool Company.

There was another problem with EDSAC: with its 3,000 valves, it was not very reliable. When it broke down, the engineers would simply replace valves one by one until they found the dud, a tedious and time-consuming process. For the Cambridge mathematicians who were its principal users, this was not a very serious problem. If the computer can do a job that would otherwise take you weeks to do by hand, then it makes little difference to you whether it does the job on Monday or Wednesday. Pinkerton, however, knew from the first that this would not be good enough for Lyons. If the computer was to take on the payroll, for example, it would have to produce payslips on time, every week, without fail. How to achieve this with such an inherently unreliable machine was the challenge facing Pinkerton and his team of engineers. Pinkerton was not afraid to ask for sufficient resources for the job. 'Any degree of reliability can be achieved if sufficient time and money are spent,' he wrote in a report in May 1949. 'My personal view is that a bold approach to the economic problem is likely to pay the best dividends in the long term.'

Pinkerton decided that for ease of maintenance he would make the computer out of interchangeable units. Each unit could hold up to 28 valves, with their associated circuitry. The units slid easily in and out of metal racks holding up to 12 units each. All the wiring, carrying both the power supply and the electrical connections from one unit to another, was threaded through the racks. Connecting the units was a matter of screwing together the contacts on the end of the pulse leads. If a unit failed, there was no need to mend it *in situ*: it was the work of a few moments to remove the whole unit and replace it with another.

The engineering team, now up to a grand total of half a dozen, very quickly realised that there was so much work to do designing and testing units that, like the mercury delay lines, they would have to be manufactured by an outside supplier. Wayne Kerr Laboratories undertook the work of wiring the units, promising to complete them by May 1950 – a hopelessly over-optimistic estimate as it turned out. The Lyons engineers tested each unit exhaustively as soon as it arrived, frequently having to return them for modifications. The job of liaising with Wayne Kerr fell to Ernest Kaye, an ebullient electronics engineer Thompson had recruited from the Research Laboratories of the General Electric Co. to be Pinkerton's chief assistant. Kaye was grappling with the unsatisfactory nature of the subcontractor's performance when an unexpected opportunity arose.

'My best friend happened to be the director of Camper & Nicholson, the boatbuilders on the South Coast,' he recalls. 'I was visiting one day and he said "You wouldn't know anyone who wanted any electrical work done, would you? We've got teams of electricians and during tough times they're sitting twiddling their thumbs." So I took him down a unit and asked him for a quote for making a similar one, and it was about half the cost of Wayne Kerr.' So the boatbuilders became part-time computer engineers, and C&N Electrical became a much bigger operation largely on the basis of the work that Lyons gave them. When Camper &

Nicholson were not making units for LEO, they were just as likely to be fitting out the Royal Yacht. Kaye recalls the consternation when a telephone call for a visiting C&N director at Cadby Hall turned out to be from Buckingham Palace.

Given the calibre and dedication of Pinkerton and his team, the task of producing what was essentially a copy of EDSAC was not intrinsically difficult, and they completed it within two years. The real challenge for the engineers was to build the additional parts of the system that EDSAC did well enough without. The difference between what Lyons needed and what could be provided by a scientific computer had been recognised by Thompson and Standingford right from the start, and carefully explained in their report: 'This system is fairly satisfactory for involved mathematical calculations when the computer has to carry out a sequence of operations that may take a considerable time (even hours) after the initial information has been inserted ... But the same advantages would not be obtained in the commercial office where the problem is to carry out a large number of simple calculations.'

What was needed were high-speed methods of delivering data and programs to the machine, and of producing the results. There would be little point in building, at great expense, a machine that could carry out a large number of simple calculations at electronic speeds if the data which the machine was to manipulate could be fed to it only much more slowly. Similarly, it would be wasteful to keep the computer waiting for its next job while the results of the previous calculation were slowly printed out.

Thompson and Standingford had thought the answer might lie in recording the input and output data in binary form on to spools of magnetised wire, a technology that had been used for some time to record sound for broadcasting and was actively being researched both at Harvard and the Moore School during their visit. The spools could be wound back and forth at a speed much greater than traditional punched tape.

The man and his brainchild: John Simmons's portrait was
superimposed on the body of the engineer Ray Shaw in this
photograph presented to Simmons at the celebratory Trocadero
dinner held in 1951.

Two years later Pinkerton and Thompson were still pursuing
this idea. They had already decided that to deal with the complexi-
ties of programs such as payroll they would need more input and

output channels than the Cambridge EDSAC's one of each. LEO was going to need three inputs and two outputs at a minimum. They concluded that the sensible thing to do would be to develop the necessary equipment in partnership with a company that had relevant experience, and chose the communications company Standard Telephones and Cables. STC were keen to be involved. Its engineers suggested using magnetic tape which, they said, had several advantages over wire. They undertook to develop tape drives that would load data into the computer at high speed, converting it from decimal to binary notation in the process, and similar output devices that would link to printers or card punches. Lyons was assured that these would be delivered by May 1951, when the whole system was due to go into operation.

By the end of 1950, when the racks were nearing completion and the memory batteries well under way, it was clear that the devices STC had promised were far from ready. Pinkerton made several visits, and discovered that there were two problems. The first was mechanical – the company had not discovered a way to stop and start a spool of tape running at high speed with sufficient accuracy. More seriously, the decimal–binary converter was simply unreliable. Despite its promises, STC was essentially using its contract with Lyons to fund a series of experiments – and the experiments were failing disastrously. Nevertheless, the Lyons directors were sufficiently encouraged by progress on the other aspects of the project to host a dinner for the LEO team at the Trocadero in May 1951.

Pinkerton continued to hope that STC would sort out their problems, but in the meantime the pressure was building up at Lyons to see the computer working. He decided that in the short term they should use tried and tested technology, paper tape or punched card readers, as the basis of slower speed inputs and out-puts. With the addition of buffers, in the form of short delay lines, to take up the slack between the slow input and output devices and the fast computer, he thought that the computer could undertake at least some clerical tasks. As long as there was an expectation that the magnetic tape units would eventually arrive – and work – no one wanted to prepare important tasks such as payroll for the slow-speed system.

On the other hand, the programmers were desperate to run something other than the test programs beloved of the engineers, to demonstrate the worth of the machine to the company. David Caminer chose a job known as Bakery Valuations, because it made relatively low demands in terms of the volume of data to be introduced to the machine, yet it would still produce information that was useful to managers. It involved calculating the value of the week's output of bread, cakes and pies from the Cadby Hall bakeries, taking into account materials, labour and indirect costs such as the power to run the ovens; calculating the value of bakery products leaving the Cadby Hall site for distribution to grocer's shops, teashops, restaurants or private customers in terms of factory costs, retail price and profit margin; and calculating the value of the products held in stock. This process was conventionally done as three separate operations, occupying fifty hours of clerks' time per week.

Caminer specified the requirements of the job, and drew up a flow chart to show how the different parts of it related to one another. Charting was developed to a fine art by Caminer and Hemy, providing a tool that clarified the logic involved, and a valuable means of checking that programs were following that logic. This part of the operation owed nothing to the influence of David Wheeler and the EDSAC team. They had seen no need for flow charts for mathematical computations; in Cambridge, preparing programs was simply a matter of translating a series of mathematical expressions into the order code, which any competent mathematician could do. The situation David Caminer faced at Lyons was very different.

'Here we were doing it for the users, with more exceptions, more ifs and buts,' he says. 'So we decided that everything should be charted meticulously, and laid down absolute standards for the charting.'

There would be the main chart of how the different parts of the program fitted together. Then there would be charts of how the major parts of each program ran within themselves, and finally a little chart showing how each stage of the process worked. Caminer had used such charts informally in Systems Research before the advent of the computer, and believes Lyons was the first company to use charts in that way. 'I was at particular pains to make sure the charts were understandable by ordinary people,' he adds. 'First of all for the person who was going to write the code; secondly for someone who was going to alter the code; and thirdly to be explained to the users on the ground. We didn't want anything to be mystical.' The charts were maintained by Joan Hyam, Caminer's secretary, who also had the job of punching the tapes of data for the early programs.

The job of writing the Bakery Valuations program itself went to John Grover, with assistance from Tony Barnes, 'sometimes leading, sometimes restlessly in step' in David Caminer's words. It ran successfully for the first time on 5 September 1951, but only as an experiment. Less than three months later rehearsals were over, and it was time to launch the new program as an integral part of Lyons's management system. On Thursday, 29 November 1951, LEO took over Bakery Valuations from the clerks who had previously done the work, and became the first computer in the world to run a routine office job.

For the rest of the life of the machine, LEO printed out weekly reports to be incorporated in the trading analyses delivered to Geoffrey Salmon, the director in charge of the bakeries. Using the slow-speed inputs and outputs, all that Lyons had available for the first year or two, it did the job in less than five hours, plus eight hours to punch the data on to paper tape. This performance, as LEO's designers and programmers were well aware, was far from state of the art. But the successful Bakery Valuations job demonstrated that a computer could be relied on to work week in, week out, not exactly without fail but with failures kept to a manageable level. And they knew what needed to be done to build up to the speeds that would be necessary to make bigger jobs such as the payroll worth doing. It was, at least, the end of the beginning.

5

LEO goes to work

For all his public austerity, John Simmons soon allowed himself to recognise that the LEO project was momentous, and that he personally had set in motion events that would change history. In 1950 – a year which, he noted, 'seems like (even though it is not) the beginning of a new half-century' – he began a handwritten chronicle, explicitly written with posterity in mind.

I think we may be on the threshold of important events in office management and therefore it might be worth while trying to chronicle them as they occur in the hope the chronicle might prove interesting in time to come. The principal reason for this is obvious enough – namely that we are well and truly embarked upon the construction of LEO, the Lyons Electronic Office, and if this venture is a success it is bound to have a profound effect . . . It is as if I were at a watershed having for years been climbing the slopes, sometimes steep, leading to the source of good organisation as I have, bit by bit, conceived it. Now we have in a measure attained it, only to be confronted with the inconceivable possibilities introduced by LEO, which may, if we dare to venture, lead us – God knows where.

But Simmons kept his musings private as long as LEO had still to prove his audacious initiative had been worthwhile.

Raymond Thompson, who was responsible for the day-to-day management of the project, began to believe that its success could have commercial implications beyond improving Lyons's accounting and management practices. It was a matter of pride to him that

Lyons was taking a lead, both in the technology and its application, and he wanted that lead to be maintained. For fear of giving away information potentially useful to other computer manufacturers, he discouraged his colleagues from publicising the progress of the computer too soon.

Derek Hemy found this position frustrating and incomprehensible. 'In 1952,' he says, 'there were some visitors from the US, I think from UNIVAC, who remarked that Lyons was about five years ahead of US development. That was a most unfortunate thing for Lyons to hear. Thompson was pathologically afraid that others would hear what we were doing and would crib. There were a number of us, Lenaerts and I included, who wanted to publish – we thought that the only way you stay ahead is by being better. But it was not allowed.' Thompson even frowned on informal discussions with others in the computing field, though that did not stop Hemy and Pinkerton from attending the occasional colloquia organised by the Computing Lab in Cambridge.

Caminer's recollection is different. With so many problems to solve in the course of inventing systems design from scratch, he was just too busy to worry about what others might be doing, or about staking LEO's claim to be first in the field. There was certainly no sense, to his mind, of looking over his shoulder in case a rival should overtake. Pinkerton seemed equally unconcerned about others' progress. 'We were neither encouraging other companies to find out what we were doing or taking a great deal of trouble to find out what the other companies were doing,' he told Chris Evans of the National Physical Laboratory in 1975, 'I think because we had the slightly big-headed idea that we were ahead anyway.'

Whatever the reason, none of the LEO pioneers publicised what they were doing until the project had been under way for several years. Others in the field seemed ignorant of their progress. For example, in a popular book on computers published in 1953 by Sir Vivian Bowden of Ferranti, neither his chapter on EDSAC nor the one on commercial applications included any mention of LEO (although this could, of course, have been wilful blindness towards a potential rival). The only form of publication Thompson would countenance – and this was with the aim of protecting Lyons's innovation – was an application for patents. Thompson ensured that the company applied for patents on various aspects of the design, particularly the input and output devices developed in association with STC, although ultimately none of their patents was upheld.

Lyons was ultimately to play a key role in showing the novelty-shy British commercial user what computers could do if properly integrated into the management of a company. But at first, as news of LEO's commissioning leaked out, probably through informal exchanges with academic supporters such as Hartree and Wilkes, it was the scientific computer users who began to queue up to ask for time on the machine. After all, LEO was a precious resource: it was one of only three working computers in Britain at the time. The first letter came to Thompson a week before the Bakery Valuations job went into routine service. The Ordnance Board of the Ministry of Supply offered £300 for work on the same problem that brought ENIAC into being and provided the impetus for many other defence computers – calculating shell trajectories. Thompson replied that although the sum was too low for the work involved, Lyons would accept the offer because it would 'provide us with experience in operating the machine on a different kind of work'.

Unlike business programs such as payroll, mathematical jobs such as ballistics calculations did not demand high-speed input and output mechanisms in order to use the computer's powers efficiently. Programming was relatively straightforward: the Cambridge Maths Lab had developed a library of 'mix and match' program components called subroutines, stored as punched paper tape, that could take care of most mathematical calculations. Hemy and Fantl made good use of these. Each night LEO would be encircled by a red tape while it ran the defence-related programs; only those who had signed the Official Secrets Act were allowed near the computer as long as they were running. Within a year LEO was also working on weather forecasting for the Meteorological Office, tables of annuity values for the Institute of Actuaries and guided missile trajectories for De Havilland. It was not what LEO was designed to do but at least it meant that the computer was running and beginning to earn its keep.

The extra work called for more programmers. During 1952 two more had joined Hemy's team, again recruited by putting the word around Lyons' clerical staff. In order to make the selection, Thompson devised a 'computer appreciation course', a gruelling week of daytime lectures and evening written assignments to test candidates' understanding. One of those to make it through the first course was Mary Blood (Mary Coombs after her later marriage to another LEO programmer), daughter of the aptly named Lyons company medical officer, William Blood. After graduating in modern languages and spending a year in Switzerland, she had reluctantly accepted temporary clerical work in the Lyons offices while she looked for something better. Despite having chosen to study French she was adept at mathematics and was soon transferred from Ice Cream Sales to the Statistical Office. It was here that she heard that the computer group was looking for programmers.

'I'd heard about LEO and was fascinated, so I leapt at the chance to go on this appreciation course,' she says. 'There were about a dozen of us, including other girls besides me, but I was the first woman to be offered a job as a result, so I felt rather pleased with myself.'

The second recruit, who attended the same appreciation course but did not join the LEO team until some months later, was Frank Land. Land, like Fantl, had come to the United Kingdom as a refugee, arriving from Germany in 1939 at the age of ten. He came to Lyons as a statistical clerk after obtaining a degree in economics from the London School of Economics. After struggling through the homework set each evening on the appreciation course with the help of his wife Ailsa (who later became a professor at the LSE), he heard that he too had been selected. Further training for Blood and Land was a matter of 'sitting next to Nellie' – in this case John Grover – who initiated them into the mysteries of binary arithmetic and supervised their early efforts. With the computer still not fully operational, much of the early work was on test programs. 'The engineers found us invaluable in helping to find faults,' says Coombs. 'I remember spending hours and hours in the computer room – you could make little loops of instructions and put them in manually straight from the control desk. There was one fault that took us hours to track down – and it turned out to be electrical interference from the lift in WX Block, the building in which LEO was housed. It didn't come out as a crackle like on the radio, it came out as something going wrong with a calculation.'

The challenge with a valve-based machine was to try to keep it running without breakdowns. A critical measure of the performance of any computer was the 'mean time between faults' – a statistic that was measured in minutes or hours rather than days. Apart from constructing the machine so that faults could be quickly traced and repaired, John Pinkerton and his team of engineers developed a system of forcing it to reveal its weaknesses every day before starting to run the jobs on that day's schedule. The first hour after switching on was automatically devoted to maintenance and testing, following a set of procedures developed and supervised by Ernest Lenaerts.

Almost half of all faults were due to valves failing, with mechanical failures in the card readers, tape readers or printers accounting for another quarter. Bad electrical connections, known as 'dry joints', were a third problem. No valve went into service in LEO without exhaustive testing in advance. All 3,000 were carefully tracked in a log book that recorded the date they were installed, the date they failed, and the reasons for failure. Lenaerts also ran a continuous program of retesting, so that every valve came up for a health check every six months or so. But testing individual valves was no substitute for testing the whole machine. Accurate calculation depended on absolute precision in the way pulses were generated and sent on their way around the circuits. Too small, and they would fail to carry the right value or instruction. 'Breakthrough' pulses in the wrong places would generate wrong answers.

The daily testing of the computer involved running programs designed to show up such faulty circuits. And to make doubly sure, the engineers ran these tests at higher and lower voltages than those at which the machine would normally operate. By stressing the system in this way they gained a good idea of the safety margin within which the computer should operate that day. This system of 'marginal testing' was also in use at Cambridge, where the Mathematical Laboratory had a similar need to keep up a high rate of reliable working, and it became standard practice throughout the industry until the much more reliable transistor-based machines replaced the early valve models.

By January 1952 LEO was operating more reliably than John Pinkerton could have dreamed when he first took on the job of building the machine. That month, the programmers ran a real test of the computer's reliability. The engineers turned LEO on, warmed it up and ran the usual test programs. They then loaded a program, which happened to be the program that calculated a table of pay-as-you-earn income tax rates, and ran it repeatedly for fifty-nine hours, during which LEO broke down fourteen times, needing a total of three and a half hours for repairs. They calculated the operational efficiency as 87 per cent – something to boast about when anything over 50 per cent was still considered good going.

At last Simmons began to think about introducing LEO to the

Ernest Lenaerts and Derek Hemy record the success of
LEO's 1952 reliability test.

wider world. He reported to the Lyons board that Wilkes believed
interest in 'the use of electronic calculators for commercial work'
was growing, and that he thought Lyons should make a public
statement before American companies started making claims
about the suitability of their own systems for office work.
Simmons therefore proposed to hold a press demonstration 'as
soon as possible'.

Unfortunately he had not anticipated the ultimate failure
of STC to build reliable tape decks, to provide the high-speed
inputs and outputs that were essential to the LEO concept. Without them LEO was a perfectly good computer for traditional
mathematical purposes but could make no claim as an economical
alternative for large-scale clerical work. The project had built up
such momentum on the systems side that to stand still was unbear-
able. Early in 1952 David Caminer proposed running a small-scale

payroll program using a mixture of conventional slow-speed inputs and the higher speed paper tape readers that were becoming available. He argued that to do so would give valuable operational experience; but tellingly, although he now denies that the LEO team saw themselves as being in any kind of race, he added in a note to Simmons: 'It should ensure that LEO is the first full-scale electronic calculator to complete a payroll.'

In October the same year the team faced the reality that the STC equipment would never work, and launched what was known euphemistically as the 'Consolidation' project. The plan was to equip LEO with three input channels (one for paper tape and two for punched cards) and two output channels (a printer and a card punch), all being implemented through the latest and fastest models of electromechanical equipment. The paper tape readers from Ferranti were similar to those used on that company's own Mark 1 computer; they were photoelectric and much faster than earlier models that used metal contacts to detect the holes in the tape. The card reader, punch and printer were all mechanical units produced by British Tabulating Machines as part of their normal punched card installation. Pinkerton took on the task of designing the input and output circuits so that they all operated independently and simultaneously, with buffer stores in the form of short mercury delay lines to iron out the difference in speed between the mechanical devices and the computer's electronics. That way the computer would never be kept waiting for data, nor would it have to wait for the output to print before going on to the next part of the program.

There was a lot of time to make up. Simmons had originally hoped to have LEO working for Lyons during 1951, but the problems with the STC equipment caused frustrating delays. The magnetic tape experiment was eventually abandoned altogether in the summer of 1953, and Simmons asked STC to dismantle and re- move their equipment. Meanwhile the engineers and programmers worked flat out to get the new input and output mechanisms installed and working. 'We were working all hours,' says Mary Coombs, recalling that when they worked late even the most junior programmer was allowed the privilege of dining in the Lyons managers' mess. LEO was eventually pronounced finished on Christmas Eve 1953. Not only was the computer complete, with smart blue doors concealing the racks of valves, but the room was decorated and ready for use. The Lyons board threw a party in No. 1 Dining Room at Cadby Hall to celebrate.

Immediately the new machine began to show its paces. The first job to benefit from the completed machine was the payroll, initially for the Cadby Hall bakeries. Payroll had been seen as an important use of the computer from the earliest days, and the payroll program had been carefully developed since Hemy's first, disappointing effort on the Cambridge computer in 1949. From the start, Thompson had specified that the computer should take no more than three seconds to calculate each worker's wages and print the payslip. In the event it took one and a half seconds. As well as printing the payslip, showing the appropriate deductions for National Insurance and income tax, and repayments on loans from the company, it took account of holiday and sick pay and performed an analysis of all the coins that would be needed to fill the pay packets, rounded to the nearest half crown (12½p).

From the middle of 1953 LEO began to shadow the work of the wages clerks, producing payslips for a few bakeries at a time. The actual payments were made using the manual system until, on 12 February 1954, LEO was judged to be reliable enough to take the task on. From that week onwards it successfully paid the wages of all the Cadby Hall bakery staff. In the next few months the number of Lyons workers whose pay was calculated by LEO went from fewer than 2,000 to nearly 10,000, the maximum that Simmons was prepared to allow until there was a standby computer. Neither it nor any of its successor machines ever failed to produce the payslips on time. Entrusting such a crucial part of the operation to a new computer could have been seen as a gamble.

The complete LEO I installation at Cadby Hall: on the left are peripherals such as the card feed, card punch, printer and paper tape readers, on the right the racks of valves and (beneath the raised floor) the mercury delay line storage.

But the months of testing and parallel running were designed to reveal any unexpected flaws, and to refine the system until it could deal with any eventuality – or almost. 'Only a few weeks after it started, the weirdest of cases came up,' recalls Derek Hemy. 'A man was going on Territorial Army leave, which did not count as annual leave. Then while he was on duty he wanted to move his holiday so it came after. Then he reported sick. I was very proud of my program, because the computer reported that it could not do this man's payslip, printed out what information it had and left it to someone else to do it. I thought "There's my boy!"'

LEO Goes Public

At last Lyons had something that Simmons thought was worth showing. As a curtain-raiser, the LEO team had turned out in strength at the third international conference on Automatic Digital Computation held at the National Physical Laboratory in Teddington in March 1953. This was the first time they had officially presented their work to the computing community, and made the case for business computing in public. In his opening address to the conference, the Cambridge professor Douglas Hartree went out of his way to highlight LEO as 'the first high-speed automatically sequenced machine to be built primarily for commercial and clerical work'. Thompson and Pinkerton each gave papers on LEO's design and operation. There was nothing else on the agenda about computers in business. The engineering director of IBM, John C. McPherson, was among the participants.

LEO went fully public almost a year later. A week after the payroll program began running, in February 1954, Lyons held a press conference and demonstration to introduce LEO to the world. The response was enthusiastic. From the *Evening News* ('Puzzled? LEO the Brain will do your thinking for you') to the *New Statesman* ('Into the industrial field has come a vast new array of workers – the slave electrons which do not pay union dues'), the local, national, daily and weekly press gave generous space to the new development. Most opted for the gee-whizz angle, focusing on LEO's perceived capacity to outdo the human brain; only a couple of the more left-wing publications muttered about clerical jobs being threatened. In a remarkably prescient aside, Ritchie Calder in the *New Statesman* speculated that if it were possible to replace valves with transistors – much more compact and reliable, but then still at an early stage of development – 'an electronics enthusiast can conceive a "cub" Leo as a desk computer'. Freed from secrecy at last, Pinkerton, Kaye, Lenaerts and Gordon Gibbs

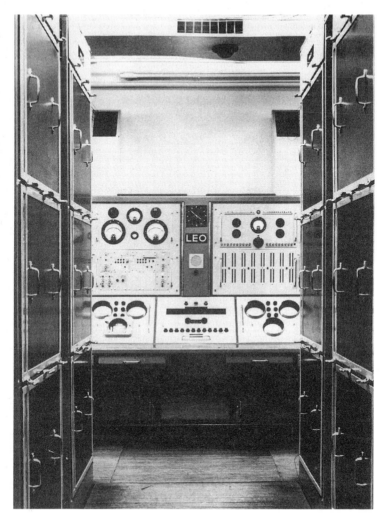

The LEO operator's console, viewed between completed racks.

wrote an award-winning series of papers for the journal *Electronic Engineering* on the design and operation of the computer and associated equipment such as the checking device for paper tapes.

The coverage of LEO for the first time brought into millions of homes the idea that computers could do the kinds of jobs that ordinary people did every day. While other computers, such as ENIAC and the Manchester Mark 1 computer, had had their share of publicity, they were seen largely as tools for mathematicians and scientists, and therefore unlikely to have much impact on the wider community. LEO was different, and inspired conflicting reactions. LEO's senior engineer Ernest Kaye remembers enthusiastically describing the project to an Austrian friend of his parents, happily outlining the work LEO could do and how it would make the drudgery of clerical work a thing of the past. 'She listened very carefully, and at the end of it she said "But we must destroy it!" And my wife thought I was going to get up and hit her.'

What of the Lyons employees, whose jobs might have been at risk? The workforce was not unionised, but there was an active staff association, and the Lyons board took a paternalistic attitude to those it employed. Everything employees needed to know about Lyons was set out in a well-produced handbook, including chapters entitled 'Your Well-being' and 'Social Amenities'. It gave details of health care services including physiotherapy, chiropody, ophthalmology, convalescent homes and dentistry as well as a full-time medical officer, all available either free or at low cost. It described the 100-acre Lyons Club at Sudbury Hill, where there was a swimming pool, cricket pitches, football pitches, tennis courts, a running track, theatre and ballroom. It advised those who had seen more than a minimum three years' service that they were entitled to a free wedding cake if they should marry. Over and above the published conditions of work, it was well known that board members had taken a personal interest in employees who fell seriously ill, and provided financial support to the widow of one Lyons worker when her husband died unexpectedly.

The LEO team also enjoyed the board's avuncular attentions. They were treated to formal dinners at the Trocadero in 1951 and the Cumberland Hotel in 1954 (both among the grander

All smiles: David Caminer (standing) shares a joke with
(left to right) John Simmons's wife Muriel, Anthony Salmon,
Jackie Caminer and Anthony Barnes at a dinner to celebrate
LEO's successful operation.

establishments in the Lyons empire); the chairman himself hosted
these events, each with its own specially printed and illustrated
menu, the bill of fare set out in French. Dinner was followed by a
cabaret featuring leading entertainers of the day: 'Shirley Abicair
and Howard de Courcy'. These marks of recognition meant a great
deal to the hard-working LEO designers, and the events were
carefully noted in the 'LEO Chronicle' kept by Thompson to
record significant developments in the history of the project.

Of course, the board could take radical decisions about staffing
if they thought the company was at risk. For example, they continued the wartime expedient of self-service in the teashops even
after the war was over, despite the public affection in which the

Nippies had been held, and the marketing advantage they had offered in the past. This was the only sensible course to follow in the post-war labour market. Although it was a time of austerity in terms of material goods, there was full employment as successive governments sought to reinvigorate the economy, conscripting men to work in the coal mines, for example. Compulsory national service continued to absorb two years of the working lives of most young men. Women's employment in occupations such as bus driving and agriculture fell as they gave up their wartime jobs to returning soldiers; at the same time, young women typically saw paid work as something one did only until one married.

In such an environment, Lyons could reasonably look forward to the labour savings promised by the computer. At the same time, its managers were unlikely to see widespread fear about redundancy as conducive to productive effort. For his part, John Simmons felt it was essential that, if the computer was to be accepted throughout the organisation, staff should feel it was there to help them, not to supersede them. He approached the problem with characteristic humanity. From the moment the board gave the go-ahead to build the computer he took the workforce into his confidence, briefing the staff on the LEO project and holding demonstrations for everyone from board members to clerical staff and even the spouses of staff involved in the project.

These demonstrations became a particular speciality of Thompson, who planned and scripted them to the last second. A natural showman, he delighted in putting LEO through its paces in front of parties of visitors – first taking the precaution of arranging for the engineers to put a secret signal in the window of the computer room to show if the computer was running smoothly or had ground to a halt. The first such demonstration was held in March 1950, when all there was of LEO was a few units capable of carrying out binary addition, but with no memory and no automatic inputs or outputs other than an oscilloscope screen.

A year later, with many more racks in place but still no inputs

Ernest Lenaerts, Ray Shaw and Ernest Kaye prepare
for a demonstration.

and outputs, LEO performed again for a single visitor – Princess
Elizabeth, who was to inherit the throne the following year. The
timetable for the day specifies that 'Mr Simmons's job will be to
explain briefly LEO, whilst walking to the Administration Block
accompanied by Mr I. M. Gluckstein . . . where they will proceed
to the second floor and the LEO Calculating Machine Room.
Here Mr Simmons will present Mr Thompson who will give a brief
description of what is occurring.' At the culmination of Thompson's demonstration LEO displayed the words 'You see I can do
it' on its screen. Her Royal Highness's reaction is not recorded.
That she was there at all was not so remarkable: she was simply on
an official visit to Cadby Hall, which regularly supplied the catering
for Buckingham Palace garden parties. By the time she reached
LEO she had already been shown the continuous choc ice plant
and Swiss roll bakery among several other departments, and still

had to meet long-serving staff and accept a toy horse and cart for the infant Prince Charles from children dressed as Nippies. It probably did not cross her mind that she was almost certainly the first representative of a royal family anywhere to come face to face with a computer.

Over the next two years, groups of staff from throughout the organisation came to see LEO in action. Thompson carefully noted the reactions of the various staff groups. In general, supervisors and above were enthusiastic and took a proprietorial pride in the fledgling computer. Some were more sceptical, regarding it as 'nothing but a toy'. The clerical staff were also sceptical, but apprehensive at the same time, taking the view that 'if it could be used at all, there were not likely to be any staff left'. Others declared – with justification – that they could add columns of figures in their heads faster than LEO was doing it.

Simmons neutralised any concerns they may have had by getting the board to allow him to promise that no one would be sacked when the computer began working. And he kept his word. In practice, the computer took so long to come into operation that normal levels of staff turnover, always high among the young women who did most of the clerical jobs, as they tended to leave on marriage, made a smooth transition from manual to computer working possible. At the same time, as the computer took on more and more work (both for Lyons and later for other companies), new jobs were created in data preparation and computer operation.

Into the teashops

Simmons's insistence on making staff feel that they were part of the new development paid dividends when he decided to introduce the computer to the most visible, but also the most conservative, part of the Lyons empire: the teashops. The teashop chain was struggling to regain the profitability it had enjoyed in the 1930s.

The first Lyons teashop celebrates the Coronation of
Elizabeth II in June 1953.

Seventy of the original 250 shops in the London area had been lost
to German bombs; no new teashop opened in London until 1951,
and nationally only twenty-four new shops were added altogether
between 1946 and 1969, while others closed.

Although they kept their trademark white and gold frontages,
the teashops never re-established the pre-war atmosphere of
luxury. The Nippies were gone for good: just as middle-class
households could no longer afford domestic servants, Lyons
found that in the altered labour market of the post-war period the
economics of a small teashop could not sustain a team of waitresses. Self-service became the norm. Formica had long since
replaced marble on the table tops, and a Lyons teashop interior
now resembled a works canteen more closely than an elegant
dining room. This impression was heightened by the poor quality

of the food. Rationing remained in force until 1954, making it impossible to produce the buttery cakes and plates of meat and vegetables in rich gravies that had previously been so appealing. The greatest selling point of a Lyons teashop meal, that it was good value for money, no longer applied. To make up for the shortage of skilled cooks, Lyons opted to prepare all the food centrally in the highly mechanised Cadby Hall kitchens and deliver it in individual frozen portions to the shops, where meals could be quickly reheated. Although they also sold ready meals in packs to the public, the term they coined for their frozen food products, 'Frood', somehow never caught on.

During the period when LEO was being developed, the teashops were beginning to face renewed problems of profitability, after enjoying a boom in popularity in the early post-war years. Frank Land's identical twin brother Ralph came to work for Lyons as a statistical clerk, and in 1953 was promoted to management accountant for the teashops division. 'In the early post-war years there was virtually no competition,' he says. 'But later on, every entertainment was oversubscribed. Football matches had 60,000 people, cinemas were full three times a week, because there was no television. The coming of television also had an effect – people stayed at home.' There was also competition from newer styles of restaurant offering fast food. Lyons itself opened the door to the hamburger by buying the rights to the Wimpy franchise in the United Kingdom. A Wimpy opened in the Coventry Street Corner House in 1953, and by the end of the 1960s Wimpy hamburger restaurants outnumbered teashops by more than two to one.

Unfortunately the management of the Lyons teashops was not equal to the challenge of these changed circumstances. In his detailed history of Lyons, Peter Bird describes the fragmented management system that was brought in as the 1950s began. Separate operational groups took charge of food production, distribution, the 'front shops' that sold tea, cakes and confectionery

By the post-war years, self-service and Formica tables had
superceded Nippies and marble.

and so on. Communication between the groups was poor. Only
the directors at Cadby Hall saw the trading figures. Advised by cost
accountants, who had never looked at how the teashops actually
worked, they took arbitrary decisions without the means to evaluate their effects. In consequence the morale of the teashop staff,
says Bird, was 'abysmal'.

John Simmons, Raymond Thompson and David Caminer saw
LEO as an opportunity not only to take the drudgery out of
managing the teashops, but also to help them improve their performance. 'It was always felt that we needed to do something for
the teashops,' says David Caminer, 'because they had the smallest
transactions of all, and had to be deadly efficient to make any
money.' But he was also excited by the possibility that LEO could
produce the kinds of figures on the performance of each teashop

and each product sold there that could enable the managers to make well-informed decisions.

Before the war the most tedious clerical job had been checking the waitresses' bills against the amounts of food taken out of the stores. It had been the awful tedium of the Checking Department that had started Simmons thinking about automatic machines twenty years before. With self-service teashops this kind of checking was no longer necessary. But the teashops operation still required enormous attention to detail in its administration. Almost every item sold was perishable. If it were not sold within a day of delivery it might be wasted; if too few of any item were ordered valuable sales would be lost. The huge chain of shops required an efficient distribution system provided by Lyons's own fleet of vans. Several different food manufacturing operations had to produce just enough supplies to keep every shop going seven days a week. It was a huge accounting task just to keep track of all the transactions – there was little capacity to analyse the figures to help the management to plan better.

The efficiency of the clerical operation had reached its limit. Representing the teashops on the board was Felix Salmon who was, according to Ralph Land, 'not by nature cut out to be a business manager'. (Land still remembers valiantly trying to teach Mr Felix the principles of discounted cash flow.) Reporting to Mr Felix were Mr Jenkins (who, typically for Lyons management staff, had begun his career as a teashop porter) and Miss Joerin. They were in charge of hiring and firing the hierarchy of regional supervisors, divisional supervisors and teashop manageresses who actually ran the operation on a day-to-day basis. The manageresses were all trained to accept nothing but the highest standard of service to customers, many of them having started with Lyons as teenage Nippies before the war. It was the task of each manageress to fill in her orders in duplicate first thing each morning in half a dozen thick form books, a separate book for each category of food: baked goods, tea, frozen food, dairy products and so on. The orders would be delivered in the next day or so, once the forms had made their way through the various departments responsible for making the food, costing it and loading it on the vans for distribution.

Very early on, before the computer was completed, David Caminer agreed with Thompson and Simmons that after the pay-roll, writing a program for the ordering and distribution of goods for the teashops should be a priority. He and Derek Hemy embarked on a study of the system as it ran at that moment. They began by leaving their offices and observing the round-the-clock operation that went on in the manufacturing and delivery sections of the Cadby Hall site.

'We went for a meal in the managers' mess,' recalls Hemy, 'and then came back down and stayed all night. At first it was all rather perplexing, with people busily rushing around. You had a series of big forms that were set out on pinboards – you had to find out what the factories should make fairly early on so that they could process the stuff, then decide what vans on what rounds should have what loaded in what sequence for which shops. Which was quite a complex business in the way of paperwork.' Caminer was also very taken with this experience of watching the beating heart of Lyons at work. 'It was a marvellous sight at night at Cadby Hall, with the lights blazing round the yard, the smell of the bread baking, and the teashop vans being loaded so that they could go out at daybreak to the teashops,' he says.

The next step was to drive around London visiting teashop manageresses and asking them what might make their work easier. These visits also gave them a valuable insight into the mindset of the teashops management. The worst crime a manageress could commit, it transpired, was to order more than she needed. 'At the end of the day if you had four rolls left that was four black marks,' says Hemy. 'So what happened? Manageresses looked at what they might sell and took a bit off and underordered.' Visiting shops in the late afternoon, Caminer and Hemy often found empty shelves.

Helping the manageresses to predict their needs more accurately would obviously help the business.

Caminer quickly realised that simply automating the existing system was out of the question. The volume of data needing to be punched on to tape for each run made it impossible. 'It was clear to me,' he says, 'that quite apart from the expense and the sheer time it would take to perforate all those orders, we would never be able to put them on to one single run on the computer.' So for days he sat with piles of orders on his desk, arranging and rearranging them and marking them with stickers, trying to see whether there was any pattern in the orders over time. There was. Caminer discovered that whether they knew it or not, the manageresses were placing basically the same orders from week to week on most of the items.

Caminer realised that by asking each manageress to come up with a standard order for each day of the week, which would be revised no more than once a month, he could massively reduce the amount of information that needed to be fed into the computer. The difficulty was that such a system on its own would be insufficiently flexible to deal with eventualities that could not be predicted so far in advance. He and his colleagues needed to find a solution to the problem of keeping the orders timely while keeping the amount of new data that had to be entered to a minimum.

The solution they found was years ahead of its time. The idea, first mooted in November 1953, was that each afternoon at a set time a data entry clerk, sitting at her card punch, would telephone the teashop manageress. Using standard numerical product codes, the manageress would tell the clerk what changes she wanted to make to her standard order. The clerk, wearing a headset to free her hands, would punch the changes on to cards as she heard them. The stacks of cards would then be sorted, delivered to the computer room and run in parallel with the standard orders. 'For the manageresses it meant that instead of spending their time with a vast assemblage of paper, they could just take a glance, pick out what they wanted to alter for whatever reason, and phone it in,' says Caminer. 'They were relieved to do their main job which was to look after their customers, which we thought very deeply about as a company.' Not only were the manageresses saved from their tedious daily form-filling, but their orders were moved several hours closer to the delivery time, enabling them to make more accurate assessments of their needs. This introduction of what was effectively online working, at a time when there were still only a handful of computers at work in the world at all, was the most obviously innovative aspect of the teashops distribution job. But there was much more to it than that.

Partly because of the frustrating delays over the non-functioning tape decks, Caminer and the programmers had time to develop a set of interlocked programs of a sophistication previously undreamed of. As well as the manageresses' alterations, they made provision for senior managers to make global alterations if there was a change in the weather, for example, or if the Swiss roll bakery had broken down. In addition, they paid minute attention to serving the needs of each of those involved in the operation. LEO took in orders listed in the manner that best suited the manageresses, and printed out packing notes in an order that made the most sense to the van loaders. It kept running totals of different product lines and printed them out at regular intervals, so that managers could see at a glance what was popular and what was not. It converted orders for portions of composite cooked dishes, such as boiled beef, carrots and dumplings, into quantities of the separate items so that they could be produced and despatched separately. It recorded the sales value of the goods delivered to each shop, so that they could be compared with the takings at the end of each month.

In principle the computer could produce statistics on just about any aspect of any part of the teashops division. Yet Caminer did not believe that there was any point in printing all of this out. It would take far too long to produce, and then even longer to digest and implement changes. So he and his colleagues built into the system the means to analyse performance selectively, on the principle of management by exception. For a range of different products, LEO could print out the ten best and ten worst performing shops. Managers would then be in a position to investigate the factors that were affecting performance and make adjustments accordingly. They could also compare advance estimates of goods required with the daily amended orders to see if manageresses were consistently over- or underestimating their future needs. In this and other ways LEO was designed not just as a fast data processor but a management tool.

As in the case of the payroll, there was no sudden switch from manual to computer operation for teashops ordering. There were several months of trial runs scheduled to begin in June 1953, before the computer installation was fully operational or the amendments began to be punched directly over the phone. The manageresses all had the opportunity to come to Cadby Hall for a demonstration of the computer's operation. Among them was Jean Cox, a former Nippie, who had managed teashops in St Albans and Piccadilly before becoming area supervisor for five teashops in the City of London. 'To me it looked like a row of kitchen cabinets,' she says. Soon though, like other manageresses, she was converted to the advantages of working with the computer. Today she comments that later in her career, when she had moved to another company and computers were far more advanced, she was never provided with the quality of information she had been able to extract from LEO.

Beginning on 24 October 1954, the teashops were gradually brought on to the system a few dozen at a time. Ethel Bridson, who had only recently been promoted from manageress to assistant area manager, was apprehensive when she heard that her London shops were to be among the first to be computerised. 'I've stepped into trouble!' was her first thought. But she was pleased to find that 'her' manageresses made the transition easily, and she appreciated the computer's advantages. 'We got everything we wanted in a much shorter time,' she says. Soon the daily reports filed by manageresses to their supervisors began to include paeans of praise to LEO. 'This is a great timesaver, work saver, and we are grateful for it,' wrote the Wembley manageress.

Unfortunately, the higher levels of management seemed less appreciative. The teashops division was possibly the most conservative part of an essentially conservative organisation. The most advanced data processing system in the world was in the hands of a management whose style had changed little since the nineteenth century, but which now lacked the vision and drive of its predecessors Montague Gluckstein and Joseph Lyons. The LEO team had designed the system that they would have liked to have had if they had been running the teashops, not one that the managers themselves had asked for. 'What we didn't manage to do, and that grieved us a little,' says David Caminer, 'was to get the top management managing as we would have wanted them to do. They still liked having their printouts of everything that was happening everywhere. People still like to look up everything for themselves, whereas the computer can do it for them much more easily.'

The other problem, from the management point of view, was that LEO's assumption of the teashops ordering job did not, in the early days at least, save money in direct clerical costs – costs were if anything higher. Even with the standard orders, the demand for data input was high. At the same time, as long as there was only one computer, a number of human clerks had to be available in case LEO ever failed. In combination, these factors meant that the overall number of clerical staff was not greatly reduced. Lyons's historian Peter Bird reports that the teashop management baulked at shouldering costs any higher than they had incurred using the previous method. At the same time the Lyons board (possibly with some prompting from Simmons, who had been an 'employé director' – one of very few non-family members on the board – since 1951) could see all the disadvantages of scrapping a system that the teashop manageresses liked, that clearly helped the efficient running of the teashops and that was a *tour de force* on the part of the LEO team. They decided to lose all the extra costs in the LEO budget, and continued this practice until clerical wages rose to such an extent that the computer gained the economic advantage.

In terms of corporate relations, it was a wise decision. While using a computer for a payroll might not seem very different from using a punched card installation, the idea of placing a computer at the heart of an ordering and distribution system was wholly novel, and Teashops Distribution caught the public imagination. The juxtaposition of the high-tech electronic machine with the homely comfort of a cup of tea and a penny bun, via the mediation of a telephone line, made for an intriguing picture. Ultimately the association of LEO with cakes was exploited by rival computer manufacturers to undermine its position, but in the early 1950s there were no rivals and Lyons could bask in the glory of its unique achievement. A publicity film of 1957 documented the whole process, from the manageress counting bread rolls in her store-room and then telephoning the key punch operators, to the computer itself reading piles of punched cards too fast for the eye to follow, and finally to the manager (pipe in hand) receiving printouts of statistics from his neatly permed secretary. Visitors treated to the full Thompson tour wrote up their experiences in admiring terms. Sir Andrew Rowell, director of the Employers' Liability Assurance Corporation, on observing the daily process of receiving amendments to the standard orders, remarked that each 'girl' had time to manipulate a cigarette, a cup of tea or a powder compact, in addition to the headphones and card punch, and added that 'the general atmosphere was one of nonchalant super-efficiency'.

6

In Business

Getting LEO built, programmed and integrated into Lyons fulfilled John Simmons's mission to replace clerical workers with an automatic machine. 'LEO leaves clerks free to use their brains to their own greater benefit and the service of the community,' he reported to a meeting of office managers in 1955. He could have stopped there, and the Lyons operation might have remained no more than a quirky footnote in the history of computing. But his evangelising instincts drove him further. As early as March 1950, he began to plant in the minds of the Lyons board the idea that their business might diversify from catering into making computers for sale. 'If the board were to decide to exploit LEO beyond the limits of the Company's own clerical work,' he wrote, 'it would be essential to set up an organisation quite distinct from any of those previously mentioned to take the initiative.' But he added reassuringly, 'This is purely speculative at the present time.'

In 1953, in a paper entitled 'Further Policy for LEO', he wrote more explicitly about the desirability of taking LEO out into the world. 'We shall be the first in the field . . . Unless we are prepared to exploit this lead rapidly we will not retain it for long . . . There would appear, therefore, to be no alternative to a determination to exploit our immediate success as soon as it is achieved and to exploit it with the utmost vigour and speed.'

From the moment the members of the board had accepted the principle of the computer, they had agreed (following the advice of their veteran company secretary George Booth) that a second machine would have to be built as back-up for the first. Computers were unreliable: if you were to manage your company with them, you needed at least two in case one of them broke down. In practice, thanks to the heroic efforts of Pinkerton and Lenaerts to pre-empt faults before they occurred, and corresponding rigour in the testing of programs, LEO I turned out to be far more reliable than anyone had expected. But a second computer had been part of the plan since 1947.

Five years after work began on what was to become LEO I, it was clear that the second machine could be substantially improved. Pinkerton now knew exactly what he was doing, and was developing a design with greater memory capacity and faster operation. Simmons's thinking was entirely logical. If the LEO team were to build a better machine, why not build two, making LEO I obsolete? And if two, then why not build more, to be leased or sold to others? There was still nothing comparable available to business users in Britain.

There was a logic to this position that the board could easily recognise. In 1954 Lyons was much more than a chain of teashops – it was among the top twenty-five British employers, with a work-force of 35,000. As well as making and selling foodstuffs, it had subsidiaries in vehicle assembly, carton manufacture, printing and laundries, all established so that the company could ensure the same high standards throughout its operations. Many of these subsidiaries supplied customers other than Lyons. Putting Lyons's clerical computing expertise on the market would simply extend a mode of operation that was already well established within Lyons.

Nevertheless, the family was understandably hesitant: the investment required would be considerable, at a time when the profitability of the core catering business was in question, and the size of the market completely unknown. Simmons persisted, however. By June 1954 he was fretting about the 'impression of amateurism' he felt that they conveyed by not being able to give a definite answer when people – potential customers as he saw them

– asked if Lyons was planning to make computers for sale. He finally persuaded the board to agree that the computer operation should as soon as possible be incorporated as a separate subsidiary company, Leo Computers Ltd. This would distance them from their catering origins and, Simmons hoped, give them greater credibility in the marketplace.

The company was duly set up on 4 November 1954. The directors were Simmons himself and Raymond Thompson (as managing director), with Anthony Salmon to represent the Lyons board. Anthony Salmon was the eldest son of Julius Salmon and Emma Gluckstein; his grandfathers were Montague Gluckstein and Barnett Salmon, two of the original Lyons founders. He had previously managed a meat factory in Fulham, and then the Lyons confectionery business. He freely admits that he had no knowledge or expertise relevant to computers; neither did he have any management training. Not until 1966 ('The day my grandson was born,' says Salmon) did Lyons instigate formal management training for the family board members. The board picked him because, owing to past experience of patent matters, he had briefly become involved in a row with STC about whether or not Lyons owned master patents on the design of the inputs and outputs for the computer. 'I got landed with the damn thing,' he says. 'Mathematics was not one of my things, but I'm very fast at doing mental arithmetic – or I was – and it amused me, playing with this idea. I was fascinated.'

So Leo Computers Ltd began life headed by the odd threesome of two Cambridge wranglers and a scion of Britain's foremost catering family. Within a month the staff of the company had been officially informed that as well as making a new model for Lyons, they would be manufacturing computers for sale. Offices and workshops in Olaf Street, Shepherd's Bush, provided a temporary home; two years later, with the first orders in prospect, Leo Computers Ltd moved into new premises at Minerva Road in North Acton. LEO was about to take its first steps out of the protected environment in which it had been nurtured, into a world of cut-throat competition in which only the fittest would survive.

In the 1940s a new word entered the lexicon of industry: automation. The word was coined at the Ford Motor Company in 1947 to describe its car assembly technology. It gained greater currency – and became a topic of hot debate – after the publication of *Automation: The Advent of the Automatic Factory* by the American management guru John Diebold in 1952. With characteristic chutzpah Diebold wrote, 'The push-button age is already obsolete: the buttons now push themselves.'

The automation debate hinged on whether automation would bring a new phase of fine living, as the optimists would have it, or return the post-war world to the 1930s horrors of mass unemployment that for many were still a recent memory. In a series of talks for BBC Radio in the mid-1950s R. H. Macmillan, a professor of engineering at Cambridge, took the more positive view, arguing that 'With the relative shortage of manpower in the West, our only hope of retaining our position in the world is to install automatic equipment as fast as we can.' This optimistic assessment was somewhat undermined when the talks were published: the book appeared with a frontispiece showing a frightened worker at a factory entrance over whom loomed a giant black robot marked 'Automation', with a threatening sky behind.

Whether because of fears of its social impact or simply because the technology was at too early a stage, offices lagged behind factories in seizing the advantages of automation. Business leaders seemed more ready to trust the work of the hand to a machine than the work of the brain. The first non-government American customer to put a computer to work on clerical tasks such as Lyons had pioneered – payroll, stock control, ordering and billing and so on – was General Electric, which installed a UNIVAC at its Appliance Park factory in Louisville, Kentucky, in 1954. By this time there were already twelve major computer manufacturers in

Frontispiece from *Automation: Friend or Foe?* by Robert
Macmillan, 1956 (with acknowledgements to *Punch*).

business in the United States. Writing in the *Harvard Business Review*
the same year, Roddy Osborn of GE commented: 'While scientists
and engineers have been wide-awake in making progress with
these remarkable tools, business, like Rip van Winkle, has been
asleep. GE's installation of a UNIVAC may be Rip van Business's
first blink.'

Business was not as sleepy as Osborn claimed, however. It
needed to be persuaded that computers would be cost effective

compared with the methods it was already using. And unless problems such as reliability and data input were addressed from the start, they often were not. According to historian of computing Paul Ceruzzi, GE had to borrow another machine at least once to run its payroll when its own broke down during the first year, and the UNIVAC often took longer to do the job than the punched card installation it had replaced. With prices so high – $1 million to buy a computer, or $15,000 to lease per month – potential business customers were understandably more cautious than universities or government departments that did not have to show a profit at the end of the year.

At the time LEO began to operate routinely in 1951, there were no truly comparable machines at work anywhere. The only two that were on their way to becoming rivals in an as-yet non-existent commercial market were Eckert and Mauchly's UNIVAC and the Ferranti Mark 1. Still in the wings was IBM, already making scientific computers mainly for defence applications but focusing its attentions in the business world on its highly profitable punched card machines market.

After leaving the Moore School in 1946, Presper Eckert and John Mauchly had set up their own company, the Electronic Control Company (later the Eckert-Mauchly Computer Corporation, EMCC). With no financial backing, they depended on advance orders (accompanied by advance payments) to support them while they built the first UNIVAC, and a smaller airborne machine for the Northrop Aircraft Corporation called BINAC. From the start it was a struggle. They charged too little for the few orders they did obtain – from the US Bureau of the Census, the Prudential Insurance Company, the market research company A. C. Nielsen and Northrop – and were constantly in financial difficulties. For a brief period their problems seemed to be over when Henry Strauss of American Totalisator bought an interest in the company, possibly with a view to making an electronic version of his highly successful mechanical calculator for racetrack betting.

But when Strauss was killed in a plane crash American Totalisator pulled out, leaving EMCC, which employed over 100 people in its Philadelphia factory by that stage, with huge debts.

There was no choice but to sell. Remington Rand, the office machines company, bought EMCC and extricated it from its commitments to deliver computers at a fraction of their true cost. With proper management in place, Eckert and Mauchly could get on with building the first UNIVAC, and it was completed and delivered to the Census Bureau at the end of March 1951. As the first commercially manufactured computer available in the United States, UNIVAC had a unique opportunity to create a market and establish itself as the market leader. Despite a purchase price of around $1 million, orders began to come in steadily, especially after a UNIVAC confounded the pollsters by accurately predicting Dwight D. Eisenhower's landslide victory in the 1952 presidential election. Models 2 and 3 also went to government customers, and by the time the UNIVAC lost out to more advanced competitors Eckert and Mauchly had built and sold forty-six of their machines.

For a brief period the company was allowed to remain the unchallenged leader in a US market for business computers that was poised to grow as fast as suppliers could meet it. But its very success stung IBM into action. The undisputed leader of the office machines market, IBM had hitherto treated automatic computing as something of a sideline, but it had nevertheless kept abreast of the developing technology. During the Second World War it had played a key role in the production of a machine known as the Harvard Mark I or IBM Automatic Sequence Controlled Calculator, designed by Howard Aiken of Harvard University.

This machine was closer in design to Charles Babbage's Difference Engine than to later electronic computers. Its calculating units were mechanically operated magnetic relays, essentially the same as those in punched card machines, and powered by an electric motor that drove a huge central crankshaft. Its programmes were not stored but read in from punched paper tape. The whole thing was over 50 feet long and weighed five tons, and worked at a rate of only three additions per second: much slower than ENIAC, but on the other hand much more reliable. It was inaugurated with great fanfare in August 1944 as the first automatic computer to come into operation, but Aiken caused mortal offence to Thomas J. Watson of IBM, then and later, by failing to acknowledge the essential role that IBM's engineers and IBM's money had played in its construction.

IBM immediately constructed a superior machine, the Selective Sequence Electronic Calculator, a one-off machine for scientific calculation. It also began to develop a large electronic stored program computer called the Defense Calculator (which became the IBM 701) that was modelled on Eckert, Mauchly and von Neumann's EDVAC design. With orders for eighteen of these machines from Department of Defense customers, IBM understandably perceived the computer as predominantly a military tool.

Until UNIVAC came on the scene, IBM had underestimated the demand for business computers: for the business market it initially produced only much faster electronic versions of its punched card machines. After the publicity surrounding UNIVAC's role in the 1951 census, Thomas J. Watson Jr suddenly realised that millions of dollars' worth of civilian business could be about to slip through his fingers, and ordered an instant change of tack. In IBM's formidably well-staffed research laboratories at Endicott and Poughkeepsie in upstate New York, business computers were given the same priority as the Defense Calculator and other military projects. By the mid-1950s IBM had launched both the large-scale 700 series and the smaller and more competitively priced 650. After 1955, although at any one time there were up to a dozen players in the market for business computers in the United States, none managed to assail the IBM lead until the advent of the desk-top computers changed the face of office computing for ever.

Initially events in the United States had little impact in Britain.

The million dollar price tag for a UNIVAC, combined with a bureaucratic labyrinth of post-war import restrictions, was off-putting enough, even if there had been much enthusiasm for the new technology among the business community. But in the early 1950s Lyons appeared to be the only business in the country that had even thought about using computers. The computer specialists themselves promulgated the view that computers were specialist tools for scientific users. The Cambridge pioneer Douglas Hartree, in a quote that has been gleefully reproduced in every computer history since, opined that the country's needs could be met by no more than half a dozen computers, administered by skilled mathematicians.

At the same time there was very little push coming from manufacturers in the engineering industry. In the United States computers were under development by individual entrepreneurs such as Eckert and Mauchly, in electronics firms such as RCA, and in office machines companies such as Burroughs and IBM. In Britain most of the technological expertise was in research institutions such as Manchester and Cambridge Universities and the National Physical Laboratory at Teddington, which were preoccupied with scientific applications and not commercially minded. Until 1949, the British office machines company British Tabulating Machines had operated as an agent of IBM, paying a 25 per cent royalty on every machine leased or sold in return for exclusive rights to the British market. In consequence, BTM had no research and development capacity of its own, despite its dominant position in the UK market for punched card machines. The agreement was terminated in October 1949, freeing BTM from crippling royalty payments but also opening up the British market to IBM for the first time.

The Lyons do-it-yourself initiative was unique – nowhere else in the world had a firm in a completely different line of business undertaken to build its own computer. That left the electronics industry, which still relied heavily on defence contracts for most of its business and was unlikely to turn to marketing computers to the business world without some external prodding.

Into this vacuum stepped the National Research Development Corporation. The NRDC was set up by the government in 1949 to encourage the commercial development of government-funded research. Its first director was Lord Halsbury, who despite his hereditary title had pursued a scientific career. At the time he was appointed he was working as director of research at the electrical and audio company Decca. Halsbury was hugely enthusiastic about computers, and saw it as his mission to create a British computer industry from the disparate pieces he found available. Discovering in his first year that there was a lot of American interest in computers but no products, he even thought Britain could earn some valuable dollars by responding to this 'snap market' and exporting computers under the noses of the US firms. With a total annual budget of £5 million, which itself was supposed to be raised from royalty earnings, the financial incentives he was able to offer to British manufacturers were limited. But in his own view, a much greater problem was the extreme reluctance of both the office machines and the electronics companies to make that bold first leap into this new field, whether in competition or in partnership.

The companies, for their part, did not quite know what to make of Halsbury. In the words of the business historian John Hendry, 'the NRDC was inevitably perceived by most firms as a threat to their independence, and its approaches were treated with suspicion'. Nevertheless, in his early days at the NRDC Halsbury represented the sum total of British government interest in computer development. Lyons, at least, was prepared to give him a hearing, even though Maurice Wilkes had previously warned John Simmons that the NRDC director thought 'any work undertaken on [computer] projects ought to be undertaken by his committee'. Halsbury first visited Cadby Hall at the end of April 1950. Simmons immediately gained the impression that Halsbury thought the Lyons team were 'well-meaning amateurs', an affront to his professional pride which he returned in his own way by privately expressing the view that Halsbury was 'perhaps rather a dilettante'. However, in true Lyons style they set out to give him a thorough grounding in the potential use of computers in the office, of which he had apparently had no previous conception.

It emerged in conversation that he was proposing to follow up Ferranti's development of the Manchester Mark 1 by persuading the company to build 100 computers for sale. Simmons was highly dubious that such a huge number of computers (at the time of their meeting there were barely half a dozen general purpose computers in the world), built without regard to the differing needs of users, could be deployed effectively. But although he believed Halsbury to be mistaken in many of his views, he thought he was sincere in his efforts to kick-start a British computing industry, and wrote to the Lyons chairman, Harry Salmon, hinting that Lyons should bid for NRDC money to help in development work.

But Halsbury seems to have been little influenced by his visit to Lyons, and no NRDC money ever came LEO's way. At the end of December 1955, by which time Lyons was committed to making computers for sale, Simmons complained to the Lyons chairman Monte Gluckstein (who had succeeded Harry Salmon in 1950) that even after a visit to the LEO factory, Halsbury would not take them seriously. 'In spite of his knowledge of and admiration for what we had achieved,' Simmons wrote, 'he cannot bring himself to think of us as manufacturers. Even though we think he was agreeably surprised by what he saw, I believe he still feels that if a job of manufacture is to be undertaken he must go to some established company.' The recipients of Halsbury's largesse were indeed all electronics firms with a history of defence-related research and development. Ferranti, as the first company in the world to make and deliver a computer (installed at Manchester University for scientific work in February 1951), did receive financial encouragement to market the machine more widely. In the end, Halsbury's plan for 100 machines was laughably wide of the mark: by 1957 Ferranti had sold just eight, only three of them to business customers as opposed to universities or defence projects. As computer historian Simon Lavington drily observed, 'When [Ferranti] started selling computers in 1951 there was no real competition: the only impediment was the inertia of the customers.' A later design, the Pegasus, also supported by NRDC and built by Ferranti, was only modestly successful, selling forty models between 1956 and 1962.

Halsbury voiced his frustration at this situation in a talk on his seven years at the helm of the NRDC, presented to the British Computer Society in 1958. 'The American user has supported the American computer manufacturer consistently and enthusiastically from first to last, by queuing up with orders for supplies,' he observed, in words that echoed Babbage's of more than a century before. 'In Britain he has hung back waiting to see a new idea tried out on the dog . . . If lack of consumer zeal is the handicap what can a body like NRDC do?'

Dream for Sale

With the launch of Leo Computers Ltd, John Simmons had provided himself with a vehicle from which he could preach the virtues of the office computer as a tool for scientific management. Even without government help, he felt he could begin the task of persuading British business to take computers seriously. A less pragmatic motive for a new and risky business venture it is hard to imagine, yet once again he managed to infect the normally risk-averse Lyons board with his enthusiasm and obtain their support. Simmons was quite explicit about his educational aims: Leo Computers Ltd was founded 'to build computers and to be the means of placing [the LEO team's] practical knowledge and experience at the disposal of others'. No doubt he convinced the Salmons and Glucksteins that Lyons would enjoy a suitable return for this apparently altruistic activity. But his aim was never to become a big player in the computer business. A year after Leo Computers was launched he wrote to the then Lyons chairman, Monte Gluckstein, that 'We have gone into manufacture not in a general way to compete with the giants, but only because we knew of no other way to get what we wanted.'

Perhaps he was being disingenuous. Going into manufacture on one's own account was one thing; making computers and selling them to others would be a very different matter. But at least at the outset Leo Computers had a good product. LEO II, designed by John Pinkerton, differed very little from LEO I in its architecture and engineering principles. It still read its inputs from paper tape and punched cards, and relied on mercury delay lines for storage and thermionic valves for its electronics. Pinkerton was able to make considerable improvements to its performance, however. He reduced the time it took for pulses to cycle around the store, from 500 microseconds to 125 microseconds, by using shorter delay lines. This development, originally proposed by the ever-inventive Ernest Lenaerts, also had the advantage that the bulky memory units took up much less space – a mere 50 feet by 25 was enough for the whole installation. Pinkerton also increased from three to sixteen the number of totals that could be held temporarily in the arithmetic unit, and the combined effect of these improvements produced a machine that operated four times as fast as LEO I. In addition, he designed it as a series of modules that could be transported separately, making it easier to deliver and install than its predecessor.

The first LEO II, begun in 1954, was supposed to be completed before the end of 1955. In the end it took almost twice as long, not coming into operation until May 1957. It was the first sign that the cottage industry approach that had built LEO I was inadequate for a manufacturer hoping to compete for sales in the wider marketplace. Lyons had accepted the principle of Leo Computers Ltd's role as a commercial computer manufacturer but failed to provide anything like enough resources. The same small team of engineers had to divide their time between R&D and production. Although expanded since the heroic effort that resulted in LEO I, the engineering team working on the design and construction of LEO II still numbered fewer than two dozen. This included stalwarts such as Lenaerts, who at the same time retained responsibility for the maintenance of LEO I. Under the less than businesslike direction of Thompson, who was constantly carried away by new ideas, they were torn in two directions. While trying to build a machine that could do anything LEO I could do (if rather more quickly), they were also having to research and develop new devices that future customers might want, such as fast printers that could print both numbers and alphabetic characters, and document readers that could interpret marks on paper and so would remove the need to punch tapes or cards.

Meanwhile David Caminer and his team of programmers had loaded LEO I to capacity with work both for Lyons and for outside customers, and watched the struggles of the engineering staff with increasing agitation. Caminer eventually put his foot down, and in a strongly worded paper headed 'General Situation', he demanded that no engineer should spend time on new developments until the basic LEO II was built. His call for reason was only partly heard. Visiting the United States at the end of 1955, Raymond Thompson and Anthony Barnes discovered that IBM had computers in production that had dispensed with both mercury delay lines and cathode ray tubes for storage, adopting a new form of memory technology called the magnetic core store. This consisted of a matrix of thousands of 'cores', each a ring about the size of a letter 'o' on this page, made of a magnetisable ceramic called ferrite. Electrical connections to each of the cores either magnetised or demagnetised the individual elements, representing the binary zeros and ones of the saved information.

Magnetic core stores had first been devised under Jay Forrester at MIT as part of Project Whirlwind, a US defence-funded project with the goal of producing a computer to control in real time first an aircraft simulator and later, as Russian nuclear capability became apparent, an air defence communication system called Project SAGE. IBM benefited from billions of dollars of Cold War defence funding to develop the technology.

Smaller, faster and more reliable than mercury delay lines, the magnetic core store would clearly be the more attractive option for future customers of LEO II. Thompson insisted that the Leo engineers devote some of their valuable time to designing a magnetic core store for the new model. But in line with the agreement on freezing the design that Caminer had managed to get through, they made the first few LEO IIs with the shorter delay lines originally envisaged by Pinkerton. Only the last four of the eleven LEO IIs that were eventually built benefited from magnetic core memories.

Thompson and Barnes's US tour had implications far beyond a switch to a new form of storage technology. They found a situation that was almost the exact reverse of what was happening in the United Kingdom, and particularly at Leo and Lyons. A radical change had taken place since Thompson's 1947 visit. Now US manufacturers, including IBM and up to a dozen others, were pouring money into the development of computers. IBM had highly impressive production facilities at its plant in upstate New York, where the visitors from Leo saw several computer systems of at least three different designs being assembled simultaneously. And there was no shortage of customers – IBM alone had orders for 100 each of two of its more expensive models. Companies such as Metropolitan Life Insurance were spending more on computer projects than the entire Leo budget.

Yet at the same time Thompson saw no evidence that anyone had successfully grappled with the needs of potential users, in business or in other fields. Some of the biggest customers, such as the Pentagon, seemed least able to specify the jobs they wanted done on the computer, and those who did use computers seemed to use them inefficiently. No one was doing regular, time-sensitive runs of data processing of the type now routine on LEO. Reporting back to the Lyons board on his return, Thompson felt able to assert that, in terms of systems and programming, there was nothing in the United States to touch LEO. 'The experts in the US have expressed the view that LEO is "old fashioned",' he said. 'On the other hand it is widely accepted that no one has put a computer into effective use except ourselves.' He went on, however, 'We must take the pessimistic view that the US will before long improve their approach to office work on computers and be in a better position than at present to install their computers effectively in England.'

Thompson's pessimism was strictly for private consumption. He used the findings from his US trip for a pre-emptive public relations strike against the American manufacturers. 'US Electronic Brain a Slow Thinker' announced the *Daily Telegraph* a few days before Christmas 1955, quoting Thompson to the effect that US companies charged £100,000 per year for a machine that was not as good as one that could be bought in the United Kingdom for £75,000. The coverage even prompted a question to be asked in the House of Commons. Commander Maitland MP enquired of the Chancellor, Rab Butler, whether 'in view of the advances towards automation made by Messrs Lyons in their use of the electronic device named LEO' the Treasury and Civil Service were thinking of using the same methods 'to enable the Nation's business to be carried out more expeditiously and more economically'. Missing the point, the chancellor replied that several computers were already in use for 'mathematical work'.

LEO goes to Market

Whatever was happening in the United States, the atmosphere at Leo Computers Ltd left no scope for doubt. A collective self-belief had grown up among the senior members of Leo staff that amounted, as Frank Land admits, to arrogance. They knew they were the first in the field; they believed they were the best. It was taken as read that every member of the team was wholly committed to making Leo a success. The *esprit de corps* that had developed among the little band who had worked on LEO I was systematically communicated to all new additions through meticulously documented and gruelling training courses that were a legacy from the Lyons style of management. It was not unusual for graduates of one training course to find themselves teaching on the next. The ethos, again echoing the situation in Lyons, was more like that of the Civil Service than of a business: unswerving loyalty was not so much demanded as assumed.

Given this atmosphere, the first high-profile departure from the company was greeted with shock and disbelief. Within weeks of the formation of Leo Computers Ltd, Derek Hemy, who coded many of the first LEO programs and trained the next tier of those recruited into the programming team, announced that he was moving to EMI, best known for its highly successful recorded music business, as one of the managers in its newly established computer division. For an able man with his own ideas, it was an obvious career move: from a subordinate position to one where he would be his own boss, and in a bigger company with more resources. Caminer was shocked that any member of the LEO team should want to leave, but wished Hemy well. To Thompson, however, a Lyons man through and through, Hemy was a traitor. Apoplectic with rage, he told him so, and snarled, 'You'll regret this.' Such histrionics simply confirmed Hemy's belief that he had made the right decision, and even John Simmons's more diplomatic offer to match the salary EMI were offering could not change his mind. Hemy went on to work with Godfrey Hounsfield on the EMIDEC 1100, the first computer in Britain whose circuits were built from transistors rather than valves, and coined the term 'second generation' to refer to computers using this technology. Hounsfield later developed the first body scanners for medical diagnosis, for which he won the Nobel prize in 1979.

Caminer was able to redeploy his other experienced programmers to ensure that existing work and preparation for LEO II did not lose momentum. But no one at the time absorbed the message that if Leo Computers was to be successful, it urgently needed more staff at more junior levels, sharing the burdens and preparing themselves to step into the shoes of their seniors. 'Strong as the chiefs were, there were very few Indians to support them,' Caminer reflected many years later. The departure of a chief was therefore a disproportionately greater loss. On the other hand, the concentration of expertise in the programming group at Leo was second to none. John Grover, Leo Fantl, Mary Blood and Frank Land had been joined by John Gosden, a virtuoso programmer who had managed to talk his way through an interview with Thompson despite the unusual distinction of having obtained a 'pass' (which, in the terminology of this august institution, means failure to achieve an honours degree) in mathematics at Cambridge. He echoes all the former Leo hands in declaring the environment unique. 'I have never worked since with as competent, bright, and stimulating a group of people. I have never since come across a group as well organised in management and systems. Later in my career I often came upon problems that were solved at LEO many years earlier,' wrote Gosden, who after leaving Leo had a long and distinguished career in computing in the United States.

The slow progress of LEO II by no means left the programmers with time on their hands. There was a series of new applications for Lyons. As well as Payroll and Teashops Distribution there was Bakery Rail Orders, which handled the orders from travelling salesmen for cakes to be distributed by rail to grocery shops around the country, even specifying the size of box needed for the order. Tea Blending was a program that valued the dozens of varieties of tea, bought either on the open market or direct from growers, that Lyons included in the various tea blends – Red Label, Green Label and so on – it packed for sale to customers. The ice cream division required a number of programs to ensure a close match between supply and demand around the country (one such program even incorporated weather forecasts). LEO I worked around the clock to meet the demand, tended by a team of operators and maintenance staff accustomed to its ways.

LEO II/1, the first of the new model to be produced, was at last finished and installed in the Cadby Hall office block, Elms House, in July 1957. It was immediately fully occupied with work for Lyons and with providing a bureau service to others. Even before the formal constitution of Leo Computers Ltd, a steady stream of work for outside customers on LEO I had been bringing in much-needed income. Gradually this became an important part of the operation. The emphasis changed from doing the odd program almost as a favour to running a service bureau both as a source of income and to advertise the merits of the computer. Working for an extremely eclectic range of customers provided the Leo programmers with valuable experience of applications ranging from complex mathematics to common business problems. Scientific work for government and defence customers continued. In 1954 LEO was employed by the Inland Revenue to print the new tax tables that would be needed for distribution to all the country's employers after the April budget – a relatively straight-forward set of calculations, but a huge printing job. No word of the figures could be released in advance of the official announcement. The chancellor of the exchequer would make his speech in the House of Commons on 6 April: as soon as he sat down a courier would set off from the Treasury to the Lyons offices. All

other work had to be taken off the machine, while the programmers and operators prepared to work through the night. That
year the chancellor made no changes to the rates of income tax,
and LEO was not needed. But the following year LEO completed
the whole set of tables overnight, a process that had previously
taken weeks by hand.

LEO was as good at this type of mathematical work as it was
at business applications, and requests appeared from a variety of
unexpected quarters. New legislation required, for example, that
the British Transport Commission maintain and publish tables of
the distances between every pair of the 7,000 railway goods sta-
tions in the country, for the purposes of charging customers. 'Staff
were calculating them by hand in a back office in Euston,' recalled
John Gosden, 'and they were falling further and further behind.'
They came to Lyons for help, and David Caminer gave the job to
Gosden. Under guidance from Leo Fantl, he broke the calculation
up into blocks, each of which could be checked by making sure
that the distances going one way were the same as the distances
coming back. There were over 5,000 blocks, each of which took
LEO twenty minutes to run. For the next eighteen months, the
computer ran a few blocks every time it had spare time in its 24-
hour-day until the job was done, generating a 'nice healthy income'
for Lyons.

The first commercial job that came to Lyons was the payroll for
the Ford Motor Company. Within weeks of Lyons announcing
that it was running its own payroll on a regular basis, in February
1954, Ford had approached the company about putting the car
workers' payroll on LEO. The program, which printed the
payslips of the thousands of workers at Ford's Dagenham plant,
was in operation by the end of the following year. It was the work
largely of four people: Leo Fantl was in charge, assisted by Mary
Blood, and much of the coding was also done by two new recruits
straight out of the five-week training course, Peter Hermon and
Arthur Payman. 'You had to measure up in a matter of weeks, or

you were out,' says Hermon. That the Ford payroll worked from the start owed everything to the stringent rules that had been established by Caminer and Hemy.

No one could start coding a program unless someone had first produced a flow chart. Flow charts had been central to the operation of systems research at Lyons since long before the computer became a reality, and today are a standard tool of programmers. Caminer and his colleagues were among the first to use charts in this way. Both the chart and the program had to be checked by another member of the team, however senior the programmer who first produced them. After program tapes had been punched (by skilled data entry staff, not the programmers themselves), a second key punch operator would repunch the program on a device that checked her punches against the first tape. The machine stopped every time there was a discrepancy, at which point the operator would correct the error.

During test runs on the computer – which were kept to an absolute minimum by the stringent checking that went on beforehand – every program fault had to be identified, thoroughly investigated and documented before the test could proceed. Anyone who let through a rare programming error would incur the full wrath of David Caminer – John Gosden remembers that he once held up the computer for four hours when he made a mistake while debugging a program, and Caminer threatened to fire him. He would personally check any written document produced within his department and send it back to be rewritten, often several times, if it did not meet his high standards of clear and correct English.

Yet no one seems to resent the hard school in which they learned their trade – nostalgia for the camaraderie of the 'goldfish bowl', as the programming room was called, is a much more common reaction. 'I've never seen anything like it since,' says Peter Hermon. 'Here you were, raw people, six months out of university, handling big business problems with Lyons's future at stake if you made a cock-up, and you were trusted to get on with it. If you didn't succeed you were out – if you did you were rewarded regularly. The senior people were always accessible – but supervision was something you sought, not something that was imposed.'

After the formation of Leo Computers Ltd, John Simmons became increasingly distant from the day-to-day progress of the company, although he was a board member. As comptroller of Lyons, a more urgent priority was to analyse the continuing failure to get back into profit of the Catering Division, which included the teashops and the Corner Houses. Despite appearances, many of Lyons's flagship enterprises had always been about prestige rather than profit. The Oxford Corner House, at the corner of Oxford Street and Tottenham Court Road, had never made a profit since its grand opening in 1928, and by 1956 the Corner Houses collectively had made losses totalling half a million pounds. The reasons were not hard to find: they charged too little for the services they offered, and they were inefficiently managed. In the words of the Lyons historian Peter Bird, 'Personal feelings and prestige seemed more important than sound commercial reasoning.' At the same time income from the teashops was down because of the decline in the number of outlets, and successful new ventures such as the Wimpy restaurants and London Steak Houses could not be guaranteed to bridge the gap.

It was against this shaky financial background that Simmons anxiously followed the progress of his own pet project, Leo Computers. His twin aims were, first, to develop an integrated, computer-based management system for Lyons that cut across its traditional divisional structure, and, secondly, to preach the gospel of computers for office work in the world beyond. For this latter task he was perfectly placed as former chairman and president of the Office Management Association, posts he held concurrently until 1950; he remained an honorary vice-president until the end of his life.

In May 1955 the Association's annual conference in East-bourne was devoted to the subject of electronics in the office. There was 'intense interest' – record numbers of members attended. Eleven manufacturers (six of them British) were adver-tising seventeen models of computer for sale at the conference. None but LEO II, as Caminer dryly noted, provided for the special needs of business customers, and none at all had yet been installed in the United Kingdom. Although interested, the audience was inclined to be sceptical. There were chuckles when, in an introduction to the workings of a computer, one lecturer quoted an anonymous salesman as saying, 'Forget the idea of a computer as an electronic brain ... Think of it as an expensive moron, infinitely slow and infinitely stupid, which can make mistakes faster than you ever dreamed possible.'

One after another managers stepped up to the podium to give their views on the prospects for computers. Some had investigated the possibilities for their own firms, then decided against. The rep-resentative of the petroleum marketing company Shell Mex & BP declared his belief that if the cheapest method was to do clerical work with quill pens, then they would use quill pens. 'The virtues of the Computer I can safely leave to others,' he concluded. The chain store firm Littlewoods was more positive: its representative reported that 'without doubt' LEO was improving the manage-ment of Lyons, but after considering the alternatives they had ordered an Elliott 405, a smaller and cheaper machine manu-factured by the British electronics firm Elliott Brothers. He bemoaned the 'general lack of fundamental knowledge relating to commercial work and the shortage of suitable personnel'. Rolls-Royce had also scanned the British market, but finding no computer ready for delivery in the near future they had ordered the new, small-scale IBM 650, which was to be installed at the end of 1955. An advertisement for IBM UK which appeared in the published proceedings of the conference in 1957 boasted that 700 such machines had been installed worldwide.

The first LEO II to be installed outside Lyons, at the steelworks
Stewarts and Lloyds in Corby.

The news that IBM was manufacturing hundreds of computers
does not seem to have intimidated the Leo contingent, who
naturally enough took a high profile at the conference. A senior
Lyons manager gave a glowing rundown on all the procedures
LEO I had taken over for the company, and Thompson con-
fidently fielded questions about the computer's capabilities. But
Simmons returned to Cadby Hall feeling that somehow they had
failed to make the impact on his fellow office managers he had
hoped for. 'They were still unable to accept the idea that Leo
Computers was really intending to manufacture and install
computers for other people,' he reported to the Lyons board.
While there was undoubtedly a general scepticism about the cost-
effectiveness of office computers, LEO II also suffered as a target

of more specific doubts about its origins. Not long after the Eastbourne conference a writer in the journal of the Association itself sneered, 'A potential computer user needs to have some confidence in his own judgement if he is to buy his computer from a teashop.'

With the arrival of its first two orders from outside Lyons, Leo had the opportunity to show the business world that it was serious. Through family connections in the tobacco business, Anthony Salmon obtained an order from W. D. & H. O. Wills, which was part of the Imperial Tobacco empire. Soon afterwards another order came through from Stewarts and Lloyds, which ran steelworks and tube-making plants in Scotland and the Midlands. With these early customers Leo established an approach to sales that contrasted vividly with the hit-and-run style of IBM. It stemmed directly from John Simmons's philosophy that a computer installation was a system, fully integrated into the operation of the business it served, and not just a piece of hardware like a punched card machine.

Once Leo obtained an order, a senior systems person from the company would spend up to three months working closely with the customer, doing everything he could to find out how the existing system worked and what the company really needed. Sometimes this analysis took place as part of the sales pitch, before the order was even received. Meanwhile a handful of the customer's staff would be sent to Cadby Hall to sit the Leo aptitude test for programmers, a gruelling day of absorbing new information and trying to apply it to real computing problems. If they passed, they would then be sent on the five-week programming course. Thompson himself gave a high priority to teaching on these courses. Once trained, the customer's staff would work with Leo programmers to write the initial programs for their company. The Leo service bureau frequently ran these until the company's own computer was ready for delivery. Training maintenance and operations staff was also part of the package, included in the bill for the computer.

This approach resulted in many happy business relationships. The Stewarts and Lloyds computer, LEO II/3, was the first to be installed for an outside customer, coming into operation in May 1958. It ran successfully until 1971, performing not only routine clerical work such as payroll, but mathematical calculations of stress and strain in tubing, and even what we would now call an expert system to predict where best to mine for iron ore. The machine for W. D. and H. O. Wills was installed later although it had been ordered first, because they demanded two novel modifications. They wanted both a backing store in the form of a magnetic drum, and an alphanumeric printer. The first, though requiring new circuits and software, was relatively straightforward. The magnetic drum store was a slow memory device that recorded information on the surface of a rotating cylinder as a pattern of magnetic dots, and had been incorporated into a number of other early computers. But a printer that could print letters as well as numbers at high speed was a new idea.

Simmons initially took the view that if you used appropriately printed forms, you needed only to print numbers, and Lyons operated that policy throughout the 1950s. What he never really understood, according to Peter Hermon, was that while Lyons employees could very quickly learn the hundred or so numerical codes that identified the company's products, other companies might have thousands of different products. Expecting their staff to memorise so many codes was simply unreasonable. But despite his prejudices, as early as March 1955 Simmons had written to Lord Halsbury at the NRDC to ask if the corporation might support Leo Computers in making trials of a fast alphanumeric printer made by an American firm. Halsbury's colleague H. J. Crawley went to the United States and looked at models from two different manufacturers, but eventually brushed off Simmons's request by saying, 'I am uncertain myself about the real requirement for high-speed printing in this country.'

Just as the abortive attempt to fit it with high speed tape drives had delayed the full deployment of LEO I, it was problems with peripheral equipment that delayed LEO II. The only high speed alphanumeric printer on offer in the United Kingdom at the time was the Samastronic printer, made by the office machines company Powers-Samas, which was an early dot matrix printer. The company advertised the machine in 1957 as having a speed of 300 lines per minute and 'a flexibility that unquestionably puts it ahead of any other machine in the world'. In response it received 200 orders almost at once: but customers soon discovered that the new device was far from ready for the market. In normal operation it could not be relied on to form the letters accurately enough. The problems of the printer sealed the collapse of Powers-Samas; it was taken over by British Tabulating Machines to form International Computers and Tabulators (ICT) in 1958, and the Samastronic printer was cancelled two years later. The Lyons engineers, particularly Lenaerts, struggled valiantly to make one work for W. D. and H. O. Wills, in order to meet their contract. But it held up delivery of LEO II/2 until September 1958, more than two years after it was ordered. Fortunately the French company Machines Bull managed to produce a much better printer that Leo was able to offer to its later customers.

Orders were coming in, but slowly. Attempts to recruit a marketing and sales expert from elsewhere within Lyons had not proved a success – if anything, it reinforced the image of a company trying to sell computers as if they were cakes. Marketing of the computers themselves, as well as the bureau service, therefore fell to David Caminer and his senior colleagues, who also had responsibility for systems design. There was no real attempt to develop a brand image for the computer, and it was some years before Leo Computers began to distribute anything like the professional and persuasive sales literature used by the IBM reps. Not until LEO II's successor, LEO III, became available did a brochure appear that used the most obvious symbol of power and performance – a leaping lion.

Simmons seemed slow to recognise that the lack of a dedicated and computer-literate marketing and sales team was a handicap to the progress of Leo Computers Ltd. When he finally suggested to Anthony Salmon, in 1959, that marketing ought to be given a higher priority, his proposed solution still seemed inadequate to the task in hand. 'We are still treating marketing as a spare time job, instead of the most important, or at least vital, single job,' he wrote. 'I suggest we ought to make it Mr Caminer's job ... We do not need to do anything sudden ... I propose that one of the programmers should be appointed as his assistant – to free him as much as possible. Then if we have chosen the right man he could become progressively his deputy and if need be, finally his replacement.'

David Caminer was duly appointed head of marketing, and given a seat on the Leo board (John Pinkerton and Anthony Barnes, who by then was head of operations, joined the board at the same time). Simmons grandly proposed that among Caminer's objectives should be 'to think of little else but how the name of LEO can be made a large and medium scale household word' and 'to make the name of LEO the first name to be thought of in the computer world.'

Nothing changed very much. The main task of selling and liaising with customers still fell to the systems design staff who acquired the title of 'consultant', and who would spend much of their time effectively working for the client company. All this accorded with Simmons's philosophy that Leo's role was not just to sell computers but to spread the gospel of the Lyons approach to using them. Unfortunately there were two major flaws in this approach. First, Leo consultants were frequently taken on permanently by the client companies, thereby draining expertise from Leo just when it needed to expand. Secondly, it had a highly detrimental effect on the bottom line. Leo never built realistic estimates of the costs of consultancy and staff training into the price of its computers.

Of the eleven LEO IIs built, the first went to Lyons, who progressively took over their own work, and the fifth stayed with Leo Computers as the core of its bureau service. In 1959 the Leo bureau opened its own office in Bayswater, above Whiteley's department store in Queensway. The new office was named Hartree House, in memory of the Cambridge professor who had given so much encouragement to Lyons in the early days and who had died the previous year. There the company installed LEO II/5, equipped with the temperamental Samastronic printer and magnetic tape decks supplied by Decca, which had at last overcome the problems that had defeated Standard Telephones and Cables a decade earlier.

The other nine machines were sold to a total of seven companies or organisations. These included the first government customer, the Ministry of Pensions, which bought a LEO to manage part of the paperwork at its huge Newcastle office. Ford bought two, as did Imperial Tobacco. The only disaster was the sale to British Oxygen. There are differing views as to what went wrong. In his account, David Caminer diplomatically mentions a 'major organisational change' that took place at British Oxygen without warning. John Aris, who as a very junior consultant was given the job of liaising with British Oxygen, has no doubt that the design of the system was the root of the problem.

A knowledge of Latin and Greek might not seem the most obvious qualification for a life in computers, but in 1958 John Aris joined Leo Computers straight from Oxford with a classics degree. He had always enjoyed the kind of mental puzzles that programming presented and he had a firm belief, as he told his sceptical parents, that computers 'would be important one day'. After going through the mill of the Leo programming course, followed by a four-month stint designing a payroll program for the Lyons teashops, he struggled for a year on the British Oxygen project. The ambitious design attempted to tackle the process known as 'explosion of parts'.

A piece of equipment, such as a soda siphon, is the end result of a series of manufacturing stages. Raw materials are made into components, which are made into sub-assemblies, which together make up the finished siphon. The explosion of parts program was supposed to schedule all the stages of the production process so that there were no shortages or surpluses at any stage. This was a job that had never been tackled by a computer before, and Leo was trying to integrate it with the more familiar tasks of keeping stock records, handling purchase orders and so on. 'The problem was not so much that the computer couldn't do it,' says Aris, 'but that we weren't able to get a real grip on the specification. We ended up with a specification that was more based on how the process ought to work than how it did work.'

Leo's consultants learned the lesson that it was vital to know who really 'owned' the system they were trying to automate. At BOC, ownership really lay in the hands of the engineers; but Leo's contact at the company was the chief accountant, who thought he knew what the engineers wanted without being fully in their confidence. It was the first time the Leo team was forced to recognise that however good their own understanding of computers and office systems, success would always depend on how well ordinary customers made use of them.

Second Generation

By the time the first few LEO IIs were delivered, the technology had moved on again, leaving them looking increasingly old-fashioned: David Caminer had been right to press for speedier delivery. The second generation of computers would dispense with bulky and temperamental valves in favour of smaller and more reliable transistors. Transistors had been developed at Bell Labs in 1948 by the physicists John Bardeen, Walter Brattain and William Shockley and had begun to be widely used in the 1950s to make compact, portable appliances such as radios and hearing aids. So began the era of 'solid state' electronics. Solid state devices perform the same functions as thermionic valves, but depend on the special properties of semiconductor materials to control voltages in a circuit. Semiconductors, such as germanium and silicon, normally conduct electricity very poorly. They can be made to carry a positive or negative charge, however, by mixing in a few atoms of metallic elements such as phosphorus or gallium. A sandwich of positively and negatively charged semiconductor layers allows a current to flow across the junction between the two in one direction only. By combining positive and negative layers in different configurations, electronics engineers could make components that linked into circuits to form electronic controls for a huge range of devices.

Why did not Pinkerton build LEO II with transistors? The advantages of transistors over valves for computer electronics were by no means obvious when he began work on the new computer in 1954, and became apparent only gradually during the late 1950s. Giving the Presidential Lecture to the British Computer Society in June 1958, Maurice Wilkes was cautious. 'Transistors will enable machines to be made smaller and more easily transportable,' he said. 'This will be an advantage, but I do not think that it will mean appreciably less overall space will be required in future for a complete data processing installation.' Computer manufacturers were relatively slow to replace valves entirely by transistors; the first devices, made from germanium, were expensive and not very reliable. But Pinkerton had used them where it seemed feasible – even LEO I included a few germanium diodes in the control of its input and output devices, for example.

By the late 1950s, with massive investment from the US defence budget, the US electronics industry had increased its capacity to produce semiconductors and improved their quality. Prices came down and transistorised computers became economically as well as technologically inevitable. Beginning in 1957–58, computer manufacturers turned their attention to designing them, and the first transistorised, or 'second generation' machines – such as the EMIDEC 1100 in the United Kingdom, and the IBM 1401 in the United States – reached their customers in 1960. They were smaller, faster and usually cheaper than their valve-based equivalents. While EMI sold only twenty-four of its first machine, the IBM 1401 was immediately a huge success, both in the United States and abroad. Its attractiveness to business customers stemmed from the fact that IBM had drawn on its punched card machine heritage in providing a complete system (much as Leo had always done). The 1401 came with advanced peripheral equipment such as a 600-line-per-minute printer, and off-the-peg business software so that companies did not need their own programmers. In terms of the performance of its processor it was not particularly advanced; however, it would come to dominate the office computer market of the early 1960s, IBM eventually selling 12,000 worldwide.

At Leo, a second generation machine was already on the drawing board before the first LEO II was delivered to a customer other than Lyons. Towards the end of 1957, John Pinkerton began to design a wholly original successor to LEO II. 'We decided that the time had come to have a complete breakthrough,' he said in 1975, 'and design a machine that would really exploit technology to a fuller extent.' While its fundamental architecture would show a family resemblance to EDSAC and the first two LEOs, the detail would be highly innovative. Using transistors, and with the more compact magnetic core store, LEO III would have eight times the storage capacity and ten times the speed of the most advanced LEO II, while fitting into a much smaller space. Its most advanced feature was the capacity to run more than one program at a time, a

John Pinkerton at work on LEO III.

facility known as multiprogramming or time-sharing. In theory it could carry out up to thirteen parallel operations simultaneously, although in normal use three or four programs at a time was more usual.

The LEO III would also incorporate microprogramming, a design feature developed by Maurice Wilkes at Cambridge. Micro-programming was a flexible way of controlling the computer's basic operations, such as the movement of a number from the arithmetic unit to the store. Each of a set of microprograms covering common clerical tasks such as 'sort' was wired into a small magnetic core matrix. Microprogramming saved processing time by reducing the traffic of data in and out of the main store, and allowed the pro-grammers to use a more elaborate set of instructions in writing their programs for the computer.

As had been the case with the two previous models, Pinkerton's designs for LEO III were informed by the needs of business users. For example, the problem of dealing with massive amounts of data on the input side and huge printing jobs on the output side could conceivably be made worse by increasing the speed of the processor doing the arithmetic operations in the middle. Time-sharing, combined with microprogramming, allowed the various data streams to be processed in a more balanced fashion.

Writing programs for the LEO III presented its own challenge. John Gosden, the failed Cambridge mathematician who had quickly established himself as one of Leo Computers' most innovative programmers and who was given the job of liaising with LEO III's builders, was more than willing to take on the challenge. For example, he had always been irritated by the binary system's inability to deal with transactions in sterling currency, without time-wasting conversion steps. By asking Pinkerton to add a further register to the arithmetic unit in LEO III, Gosden gave it the capacity to carry out 'mixed radix arithmetic' and therefore to deal swiftly and easily with the idiosyncratic system of 12 pence to the shilling, 20 shillings to the pound that Britain used before decimalisation in 1971. 'It was really a very simple scheme to implement,' says Gosden, but Leo Fantl, himself no slouch in software design, called it 'fiendishly cunning'. The same system turned out to be useful for a variety of other non-decimal quantities, such as hours and minutes or pounds and ounces.

In 1960 Gosden was headhunted away from Leo and spent the rest of his career on a variety of computing projects in the United States, including advising the White House under Jimmy Carter on its information systems. At Leo, the software developments he began for LEO III were taken over by Ernest Roberts, a mathematics graduate from Oxford who had previously worked on mathematical programs. Roberts developed the larger set of microprogrammed instructions, such as 'merge', to enable the computer to sort large volumes of data on tape without putting too much load on the main memory or the arithmetic unit, and what the Leo team called the 'Master Routine'. This was effectively what we would now call an operating system, a piece of software that managed other programs that were running on the computer.

A further innovation was a programming language known as CLEO (Clear Language for Expressing Orders) that would free programmers from the tedium of writing programs in code, one instruction at a time. CLEO was a pet project of Raymond Thompson's. A high-level programming language – one that essentially used plain English rather than codes comprehensible only to the computer – was not a new idea: IBM had introduced FORTRAN for scientific users in the mid-1950s, and a US government-sponsored committee had developed COBOL, largely inspired by the work of Grace Hopper at UNIVAC, for commercial work. While FORTRAN used mathematical equations as instructions, COBOL used English words and syntax. An instruction in COBOL replaced dozens of lines of machine code instructions and might read SUBTRACT TAX FROM GROSS PAY GIVING NET PAY. A program known as a compiler then converted the high-level language instructions into machine code.

Given that dozens of people had already spent thousands of hours working on COBOL and the compilers that went with it, why did Leo Computers want to develop their own high-level language? 'Ask my colleague Ray Thompson!' says Caminer. 'We spent headbanging sessions on these things. I could see no reason why we should go against the field.' No one at Leo was unaware of the conflict – more than one ex-Leo hand has mentioned spectacular rows between Thompson and Caminer as one of their abiding memories of their time at the company. One of Thompson's arguments was that because of its microprogramming, LEO III had a much more advanced language structure than other machines of its type. 'So the feeling was that if we used COBOL we would lose some of the advantages of the computer,' says Caminer. 'Instead Thompson argued that CLEO was the best

LEO III was the first of the LEO family to be fully transistorised.

language in the world, so why didn't we promote CLEO instead of COBOL? It was a mistake, and subsequently it became a black mark, something you had to overcome.'

Leo was by no means the only company to make this mistake. Ferranti also developed its own high-level language, called NEBULA, and across the world there was a proliferation of similar efforts, each consuming literally years of programming time.

But COBOL proved to be both durable and adaptable, and is still in use today, while almost all the others met an early demise.

There was no question that LEO III was a groundbreaking machine, and its later successes confirmed John Pinkerton's status as a computer designer of genius. Nonetheless, its introduction to the world was fatally hampered by mismanagement. As with LEO II, the design team working on LEO III was ludicrously under-staffed – Peter Bird quotes a figure of just six people, compared with the armies developing new machines at IBM. Inevitably the production schedule for the first machine, to be installed at Hartree House, ran late. It eventually began operating in April 1962, and then experienced months of teething troubles with the advanced peripherals, such as tape drives and a high-speed printer, that had been bought in from American suppliers. These difficulties were eventually overcome, but despite the excellence of the product, says David Caminer, selling it was still a problem. 'We had devised this machine which really was quite splendid,' he says. 'But we didn't do any of the things that were necessary at that point. We didn't recruit more engineers, we didn't recruit more consultants, we didn't make a business plan and say how much money we were going to need – we just dribbled along. So when we decided to launch LEO III we made no launch programme at all.'

Insofar as there was a plan, it was clearly influenced by the old Simmons philosophy that spreading the word was at least as important as selling machines. The idea emerged that Leo Computers would set up a LEO III service bureau in South Africa, jointly with Rand Mines. Lyons had a flourishing export market for its teas in South Africa, and good contacts there. Thompson was enthusiastic about this scheme and sent David Caminer to Johannesburg for several weeks in 1960 to negotiate the agreement with the gold-mining company Rand Mines and to lay the groundwork for the service bureau. Soon afterwards Leo Fantl, who had recently been widowed, arrived there to take over from Caminer, to recruit and train staff for the bureau, and, as it turned out, to start a new life in South Africa.

The South African enterprise, though it stretched the resources of Leo Computers Ltd to the limit, was a success. But from the point of view of Leo Computers as a whole, David Caminer now believes, it was another serious mistake. 'It occupied an absurd amount of time for the organisation at that point, and particularly of my own time as marketing manager,' he says. 'I sometimes wonder now why in God's name didn't I revolt about being in South Africa when I should have been holding mass gatherings to tell people about this magnificent machine that we had built. And it took one of our best people in Leo Fantl.'

Why did Leo, and its parent company Lyons, not invest more in marketing LEO III? Undoubtedly the Lyons board were beginning to get cold feet. For Leo to become a serious competitor to IBM, or even the other British manufacturers, would have taken enormous resources. Anthony Salmon remembers that his request for an extremely modest £100,000 to build the first LEO III had 'caused havoc' in the boardroom – and he got his money with the promise that it would be recouped on sales of only twenty machines. It was not exactly what you could call a business plan.

The history of computers does not bear out Ralph Waldo Emerson's dictum that if a man builds a better mousetrap 'though he build his house in the woods, the world will make a beaten path to his door'. However good your computer, you have to sell it. Making the first sale of LEO III in competition with rivals, principally IBM and the largest of the British companies, ICT, was a nerve-racking business for the Leo team, even though they knew they had a better product. The first customer was the tyre manufacturer, the Dunlop Rubber Company. Peter Hermon was the consultant who carried out the initial analysis of the extremely complex requirements of this huge business, which made around 20,000 different products. In four years he had advanced from mathematics graduate with no business experience to a senior member of the team, having designed a similarly complex system for Imperial Tobacco's LEO II and obtained an early promotion when one of Derek Hemy's first recruits, John Grover, left to join him at EMI.

At Dunlop, all seemed to be proceeding smoothly, until at the last minute, with contracts due to be signed any day, Hermon got wind that the rival IBM team had sown doubts about the viability of Leo Computers Ltd in the minds of the Dunlop management. In desperation he spoke to Anthony Salmon. 'I consulted an uncle of mine,' says Salmon, 'and he thought one of my cousins would help.' The cousin happened to be Sir Norman Joseph, then chairman of Lyons, who knew the Dunlop chairman, Sir Edward Beharrell. 'At half-past nine the next morning we had a call from the chairman to say they had bought the machine,' says Salmon. 'My cousin had the nerve to ring up the chairman at his home that night and tell them the predicament Leo was in, and by ten past nine he phoned my cousin and my cousin phoned me.' Within a short time the order for a LEO III was confirmed – but it was the old boys' network, rather than shrewd marketing, that had clinched the sale.

Leo Computers would not always be able to use its connections to the aristocracy of British business in order to win the far from gentlemanly struggle for sales. And even the success with Dunlop came with a heavy price: unbeknown even to Peter Hermon himself, he had been included in the package and left Leo in 1959 to head data processing at the tyre company. Thompson saw his departure as beneficial, confirming a strong link with a good customer; he had earlier urged Hermon to accept an extremely lucrative offer from Imperial Tobacco. But David Caminer bitterly regretted the loss of another key member of staff. 'We lost many of our best people to customers at a time when they should have been building up departments,' he says. 'Lyons thought people were replaceable. But when Leo started recruiting, only the most venturesome people were interested. We couldn't afford to lose those people. Knowing what the customer needed could not be delegated downward.' Peter Hermon became part of the diaspora of Leo-trained staff who played significant roles in the development of computing in Britain. He stayed five years with Dunlop before joining the national airline BOAC, where he developed one of the world's first worldwide, real-time, online ticketing systems. For this job he assembled an outstanding team of Leo-trained consultants and programmers, which achieved world-class results. Later Hermon became a director of British Airways.

Despite these stresses to the system, by 1960 the staff of Leo Computers Ltd could well believe that they were entering a golden age. Their numbers had increased to well over 400 in total, there was work in plenty for the service bureau, and the new product, LEO III, was widely admired and beginning to win orders in the teeth of competition from much larger rivals. Surely the new decade could bring only further success?

7

Leo's Last Roar

The report that had arrived one morning in the summer of 1962 from the merchant bankers Lazards made uncomfortable reading for John Simmons. It quoted one view that with the need to reach export markets, manufacture and market a full range of peripherals and keep new products constantly in development, no company should stay in computer manufacture unless they were prepared to commit themselves to up to £50 million of capital expenditure by the end of the decade. While conceding that this was an extreme view, the anonymous author went on to say that although a smaller operation could be successful, it was doubtful that a small computer business carried on as a subsidiary of a very different business could hold its own with the giants in a rapidly growing market. It would be up to the managers of the parent company, the report went on, to ask whether the return on capital from the computer subsidiary was keeping pace with that from the core business.

Simmons disagreed with much that was in this report, commissioned by Lazards for Lyons, but he could not dispute the fact that had driven Lyons to consult Lazards in the first place. Leo Computers was losing money: it had made a net loss of £300,000 since its foundation in 1954. As long as Lyons's catering business was booming such losses might have been tolerable. But in the late 1950s and early 1960s the company's legendary ability to pull in customers seemed to be faltering. It could no longer count on increased year-on-year profits, and the Leo figures made the shortfall look even more embarrassing.

Simmons may himself have started a train of thought within the Lyons board by suggesting to Anthony Salmon in October 1961 that Leo should give up manufacturing altogether and concentrate on its service bureaux. From the start, he had seen computer manufacture as necessary only in order to spread the message about computer use; now that computers were available from a number of other manufacturers, he saw no particular reason to continue with a sideline that showed little sign of being profitable. The same thought must have occurred to the family board members at Lyons. When one of Anthony Salmon's cousins suggested to him that they should get out of the computer business, his immediate feeling was one of enormous relief. 'I made up my mind I'd have no more anxieties,' he says. 'You've got no idea what it's like, waiting to hear whether you've got an order for £250,000. You never got second prize; you either got £250,000 or nothing. And the anxiety was something too terrible for words.'

Within months discussions began with Lazards not just about withdrawing from computer manufacture, but about a merger with one or more other computer businesses. These discussions involved Anthony Salmon, John Simmons and sometimes Raymond Thompson, the managing director of Leo Computers. They were kept completely secret from the rest of the Leo staff – including its other board members, David Caminer, John Pinkerton and Anthony Barnes. 'The thing had got bigger and bigger,' says Caminer. 'It must have seemed like Frankenstein's monster – we were taking a lot of orders, but that meant more staff and higher stock costs. Anthony started looking for partners, but the Leo board not involved – I knew no more than a mechanic with a screwdriver.'

With no inkling of what was going on in boardrooms and city offices, at the Minerva Road factory Pinkerton had been working on an upgrade of the LEO III to make an even faster version called the 326. He had an experimental model running at the factory by 1963, and the team of consultants began to win orders, often going head to head with the best that IBM could offer, on the grounds that it was simply superior to anything else available at the time. Some of these orders, for the Post Office for example, were among the largest ever placed in Europe to that date. At last it seemed possible that Leo Computers was poised to take not only a technological but also a commercial lead. Yet throughout this period its parent company was plotting a strategic with-drawal that would leave Leo without the resources to exploit its advantage.

English Electric, a large, general electrical company whose com-puter division was based at Kidsgrove, near Sheffield in the north of England, quickly emerged as the most likely target of some kind of partnership arrangement with Leo. The company, equally well known for heavy electrical engineering installations and for domestic appliances such as refrigerators and electric cookers, had entered the computer field in the mid-1950s. It had collaborated with the National Physical Laboratory in building an engineered version of the Pilot ACE, designed by Alan Turing at NPL after the Second World War. English Electric's computer, the DEUCE, was designed for scientific users and was first delivered in 1955. By 1963 the company was selling a range of machines including the KDF 9 for scientific users and the KDP 10 for commercial work. It had a long-standing agreement with RCA in the United States to share technology.

On Lazards's advice, Salmon and Simmons first tried to set up a wider European consortium involving not only English Electric but also Siemens in Germany, Olivetti in Italy and Bull in France. Leo's role would be reduced to 'sales and user research'. This plan proved too ambitious, and so they turned their attention to the possibility of a merger with English Electric alone. At this point Simmons clearly believed that whatever he was negotiating, it would leave Leo as an equal partner. 'Nobody is taking over anybody else,' he assured Geoffrey Salmon in a progress report.

Lazards – two of whose directors were also directors of English Electric – brokered the deal, drawing up an agreement between Lyons and English Electric that was eventually signed on 3 February 1963. English Electric agreed to merge its computer business with Leo Computers, and not to undertake any further computer-related activities. On paper the agreement looks like a takeover by Leo: 'To effect this merger Leo should acquire from English Electric the whole of its electronic computer business . . .' In practice the result was very different. English Electric acquired half the shares in the joint business, Lyons keeping the other half. The chairman of the new company was to be Sir Gordon Radley, former director general of the Post Office, who headed English Electric's defence and telecommunications subsidiary Marconi. Anthony Salmon was given the post of vice-chairman, but in his own words he was little more than a 'sleeping partner' from then on. He lacked Radley's technological know-how, and there was no further need for him to champion the cause of Leo among his family members on the Lyons board.

John Pinkerton and David Caminer knew nothing about the merger apart from the odd whisper until it was signed and sealed and ready to be announced to the press. *The Times* called it 'a sensible piece of rationalisation which will result in a powerful British company ready to compete on equal terms with the other big manufacturers, particularly in the lucrative European market'. The old Leo hands greeted the news with disbelief and dismay. 'There was deep emotion for our machines and methods of work,' recalls Caminer, 'and no enthusiasm for the merger.' They knew that Leo had some ground to make up financially, but in LEO III they had a machine of which they felt justly proud. Was Lyons about to throw away all that they had achieved? 'At that time it wasn't quite clear whether it was, as it was put to us, a merger, or as it turned out to be, a takeover,' says Frank Land. 'The great question was who was going to be managing director?'

Two weeks after the announcement the Leo staff were

informed that the new organisation would be managed not by Thompson, but by W. E. (Wilf) Scott, the head of English Electric's computer division. This was a turn of events that Thompson himself had not anticipated, even though he had been involved in discussions about the merger. Although he did not discuss his feelings, Caminer knew that Thompson was deeply upset by the decision. Both Land and Caminer recall that Thompson could barely bring himself to speak to Scott, and so took no further part in directing the strategy of the new company. He was given responsibility for marketing, an activity for which he had little previous experience or inclination. The same pattern was repeated throughout the company. At each level a former English Electric manager was put in either alongside or over the head of the corresponding Leo manager.

Although they were in the same business, there were huge cultural differences between the two halves of the newly merged company. English Electric had a traditional, hierarchical management structure with clearly defined responsibilities: a 'role culture' in the parlance of modern management. Its approach to making and selling computers did not include the detailed preliminary analysis of the customer's needs that had become standard at Leo. Though it had grown to a staff of almost 500, Leo had retained the 'task culture' of its early days, when what mattered was to get the job done and done well, and not to fuss too much about job descriptions or seniority. The culture engendered huge confidence among its consultants, who still combined the functions of salesmen and systems designers with their role as advisers on the installation of new systems.

The first encounter with their new colleagues only confirmed their sense of superiority. 'They were simply not at the same level of smartness as we were,' says Land. 'So we suddenly found ourselves in the position of being put in harness with people whom we felt were really below us in capability. And that hurt.' Perhaps the final indignity was the name given to the new company, English

Electric Leo, or EEL: no longer a proud beast of the savannah but a legless, crawling thing, neither fish nor flesh.

The unpromising name did not last long. Within little over a year one of EEL's parents, English Electric, was finding its original undertaking not to manufacture computers unduly restrictive. Its Marconi subsidiary wanted to be able to add computers to its products, particularly those aimed at the defence market. The members of the Lyons board saw an opportunity to recoup their investment in a loss-making activity, and sold their remaining shares in EEL to English Electric for slightly less than £2 million, mostly in cash and partly in English Electric shares. EEL thereby became a wholly-owned subsidiary of English Electric, which merged it with Marconi and gave it the even more agglutinative handle, English Electric Leo Marconi Computers Ltd. In announcing the deal in October 1964, Lyons said that they 'had achieved their main purpose of developing computers to meet the requirements of their own business, and the consideration agreed approximately covers Lyons' total expenditure on the Leo computer project since its inception'. Anthony Salmon recalls the deal as 'all very amicable' – one can imagine the smiles of relief around the table in the Lyons boardroom that they had emerged from this adventure no worse off than they began. If any board member expressed regret, it was not recorded.

There was plenty of regret, however, among their former employees. The remaining Leo pioneers – Thompson, Caminer, Pinkerton, Fantl, Barnes, Lenaerts, Coombs, Land – had always seen themselves as working not only for Leo but for Lyons. That Lyons was prepared to sell them off without so much as asking their opinion, after all the effort they had put into it and all that they had achieved, was a brutal shock.

The 'Master Plan'

How could John Simmons, of all people, be party to this? It was Simmons's vision that had given birth to the line of LEO computers, Simmons's philosophy of management that the Leo board continued to spread through their contacts with customers. But Simmons always owed his first loyalty to Lyons, and by the mid-1960s his interest in Leo was mainly that of a customer (if a rather special one) towards a long-standing and reliable supplier. As for Lyons, it had problems of its own.

With the LEO III in prospect, John Simmons had seen the opportunity to put the final touches to what had long been a dearly cherished dream: a decentralised management structure, with divisions of the company operating independently, but all served by the same, fully integrated, centralised management information system. Without apparent irony, he called his idea the Master Plan, and published it in his 1962 book, *Leo and the Managers*. The book began as a set of lectures Simmons gave on internal Lyons management training courses; publishing it gave him the opportunity to expound his theories more widely. Introducing his book, he unblushingly cast himself as the Albert Einstein of the management world: 'Not only does it describe a general theory on the organisation of business management, but it also describes a special theory on how computers should be used by the managers in such an organisation.'

He went on to tell the story of LEO's creation, and to describe the Master Plan. 'LEO is to the thinking of a manager,' he said, 'as a grammar book is to the words of a speaker. It is the embodiment of a logic or discipline, which can be self-imposed for clear thinking and expression, but which need not govern the manager, any more than the discipline of a grammar governs the freedom of a speaker ... The use of LEO brings a new freedom and power to

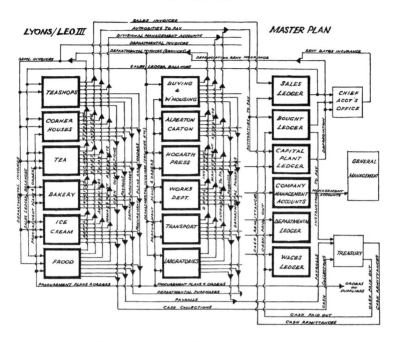

John Simmons's Master Plan for the management of
Lyons using LEO III.

managerial thinking and decision making and, again, a means of unambiguous communication.'

Unfortunately the gulf between theory and practice was as wide as ever. Jealous of their independence, the heads of the Lyons divisions proved to be unwilling to adapt themselves to the 'logic or discipline' of the Master Plan. The divisions were essentially independent fiefdoms, each with a family member at its head, all of whom had seats on the board. Not having learned the lessons of earlier applications, such as the Teashops Distribution job, Simmons designed it to run Lyons the way he thought it should be run, not the way the managers were used to running it. The elaborate plan, encapsulated in a beautiful hand-drawn chart, directed the flow of information between the main Lyons divisions (teashops, Corner Houses, tea, bakery, ice cream and 'Frood'), the service departments such as packaging and laboratories, and the various accounts departments. It was developed under Simmons's direction by the Organisation and Methods Department (formerly known as Systems Research) virtually without reference to the line managers.

Simmons initially costed the implementation of the plan at £500,000, and told the board that he expected it to pay for itself easily in clerical savings. Such was Simmons's influence that, as he had come to expect, they nodded it through. His first LEO III – with the serial number 7 – arrived in 1963, and a faster 326 three years later. Throughout the whole history of his relationship with LEO computers, Simmons had always asked for – and usually got – performance from the machine that was at the very limit of what was possible. Showing little appreciation of the task facing Leo Computers as it tried to win orders and meet production schedules for its state-of-the-art LEO III, Simmons requested two new, experimental items of peripheral equipment as part of his LEO III installation. One was a device that read marks directly from stacks of paper forms into the computer; the other was an advanced, high-speed printer that could print forms at the same time as filling them in. The computer installation would, therefore, be able to use its own output of printed forms as input, greatly reducing the time and labour required to prepare data for the computer by punching cards or paper tape.

Neither of these devices was ready for Leo to buy off the shelf; in both cases the company had to set up collaborations with specialist firms to develop them for Lyons, and hope that the precious time spent on them by consultants and engineers would pay off in the long term. The printer, developed with the Rank Organisation, was expensive and never very reliable; in July 1967 the model owned by Lyons caught fire and nearly destroyed the entire computer room. The mark-reading device took many months of experimentation to complete: getting it to pick up and feed through the sheets of paper was at least as difficult a problem as that of reading the marks. The first model, Lector, had to be fed one sheet at a time, but this was insufficiently automated for Simmons.

Pinkerton then worked with a Bristol company called Parnall to produce Autolector, which could read sheets automatically from a stack. One Leo recruit remarked that it 'looked and sounded like a combine harvester, with its welter of flying paper', but added that if it jammed it could destroy 'huge volumes of input documents which had to be carefully extracted, ironed flat and fed to the more primitive but tolerant Lector by hand'. Autolector helped to win a contract with the Royal Dockyards for LEO III, the only sale it made to a Ministry of Defence customer. Only eight in total were ever sold, however. John Aris, who was acting as Leo Computers' main liaison with Lyons, remembers that working on these devices was an unwelcome distraction for the Leo team.

John Simmons never saw his Master Plan come into being. His mistake, in David Caminer's view, was his failure to recognise that the different divisions were used to operating with a degree of autonomy and quite different 'esprits': 'Trying to bring everything together ran counter to Lyons thinking.' Staff movements between divisions were rare, and the family members at the head of each division ran them as separate businesses. They had been happy to make use of the central computing service to automate some of their clerical operations, such as Bakery Valuations and Tea-shops Distribution. Expecting them to rely on a fully integrated, company-wide system encroached on their autonomy, however; and even as Simmons strove to draw them into his Master Plan they saw a way to reassert their independence.

In the late 1960s computers became smaller and cheaper. The latest electronic technology was the integrated circuit, which con-sisted of miniaturised transistors and other solid-state components etched into wafers of silicon: the first computer chips. At the same time standard software packages for word processing, accounting or database management reduced the need to depend on a team of specialist programmers. These developments made it possible for the managers at Lyons to buy their own minicomputers rather than rely on a central service. The divisions became even more independent than before.

John Simmons retired from Lyons in 1968, after forty-five years of devotion to the company and to pursuit of the ideal office system. After his retirement Lyons set up a Computer Services Division, with representatives from all the operating divisions, and in a rather desperate attempt to recover some kind of central control it decided to buy a new mainframe – an IBM. But it was already too late – the minicomputer genie was out of the bottle and individual departments insisted on managing their own data processing.

By this time the Lyons catering business, one of the most high-profile British commercial operations of the twentieth century, was itself in serious trouble. An investigation, chaired by Simmons, reported in 1962 that no part of the catering operation was profitable other than the London Steak Houses, but his recommendation that the catering businesses be allowed to manage themselves – rather than taking directions from a distant general manager – was not accepted. Two years later he was again involved in a study group set up to explore the possibility of a new management structure for Lyons. But the new structure still left family members in charge, and the generation now in control lacked the inspired vision of their predecessors. Even if a radical plan had emerged in a board meeting, the principle of consensus was so ingrained that if just one family member disagreed it would be dropped. 'So obsessed had they become with family mystique and family mythology that what was originally a dynamic and creative force had become hardened and fossilised into a set of unworkable and seemingly ineluctable rules and regulations,' wrote Stephen Aris a few years later in his book, *The Jews in Business*.

In 1969 the teashops were revamped as 'Jolyon' restaurants.

Painful as it was, there was only one way to stem the losses from the Catering Division. The Trocadero, one of Lyons's central London flagship restaurants, closed in 1965, and two of the three Corner Houses in 1967 and 1969. In 1969 the teashops, which had been finding it increasingly difficult to compete with new fast-food chains, were revamped as 'Jolyon' restaurants, in the hope that Lyons could capitalise on the name of a character in the hugely popular 26-part BBC television series, *The Forsyte Saga*.

The change coincided with yet another new management structure for the company. Faced with the evidence of its failures, the family finally agreed to abandon the automatic promotion of its members. Although the new chairman, Geoffrey Salmon, was still a family member, as were most of the board of directors, he was appointed on merit and not because it was his turn. At the same time Lyons introduced a clear demarcation between board membership and divisional management, with divisional heads appointed on merit regardless of their family status. The changes appeared to be effective, with the company enjoying a return to profitability in the early 1970s.

However, in order to enjoy continued growth they had to find larger markets, and that meant becoming a global business. Lyons set about acquiring a range of food manufacturers in Europe and the United States, funded by extensive borrowing. The timing turned out to be disastrous. As interest rates skyrocketed after the oil crisis of 1973, Lyons was left with huge debts and had no alternative but to dispose of some of its key assets.

The teashops had for years been worth more for their high street sites than they could generate in profit as businesses. Lyons began to close them in 1977, and the last, at Marble Arch in London's West End, shut its doors in 1981. In the same period Lyons sold its prestige hotels in central London, a move that, as Peter Bird reports in his history of the company, left several directors in tears.

Lyons's obvious weakness made it vulnerable to a corporate takeover as large companies vied with one another for supremacy in the various market sectors. A powerful player in the food and drink business was Allied Breweries, brewer of Tetley's and Ind Coope beers and owners of a chain of over a thousand pubs. In 1978 it bought Lyons, changing the name to Allied-Lyons three years later. The showcase Cadby Hall food factory, where the first LEO was built, had long since ceased to supply even Lyons's own restaurants; it was demolished and sold to developers in 1984. In 1994 Allied-Lyons became Allied Domecq after acquiring the sherry importer Domecq and disposing of its remaining food manufacturing interests. The Lyons name lives on only in brands of tea and coffee, now produced by companies based in India and the Netherlands respectively.

End of the LEO Line

It was obvious that Lyons could not go on supporting a loss-making computer business when its core business was clearly in trouble. It was hard for the Leo Computers board to accept the sale of the company to English Electric in 1964, but they could see the logic once they had got over the shock. What they found harder to stomach was the failure of the newly merged company to capitalise on the technological superiority of the LEO III and 326. Indeed, the merger negotiations seem not to have included any discussion of what the new company was to make and sell.

English Electric Leo began life with a motley collection of incompatible products. The LEO III and 326 were state-of-the-art machines for commercially oriented, integrated data processing. The KDF 9 was a similarly advanced machine for scientific users, directly in line from English Electric's earlier scientific machines such as the DEUCE. The KDP 10, a design manufactured under licence from RCA, was showing its age. Frustratingly, Scott was unwilling to drop the KDP 10 even though it was aimed at the same market as the much more advanced LEO III. Inevitably the LEO machine had its partisans within the merged company, as did the English Electric machines, and Scott did little to bring about any kind of rationalisation. Frank Land, as chief consultant in Caminer's sales team, was forced to waste much of his time arguing with the ex-English Electric sales staff about which machine should be presented to prospective customers. He found it difficult to establish any common ground with their approach: there was none of the rigorous 'sizing' of the prospective customer's job with which he and the other Leo consultants had grown up.

In the event Scott's hand was forced by IBM. In 1964 IBM announced not just a new model, but a new range of computers called System 360. During the first decade of commercial computer manufacture, every company involved underestimated both how fast the technology would develop, and how rapidly users' needs would change. Large companies such as IBM might be able to offer a wide range of products, but they were not mutually compatible. At the same time buying a computer involved such a huge outlay that it was difficult to see it as other than a long-term investment. Persuading customers to upgrade from their existing model, even with the same supplier, was difficult when it meant a huge investment in new systems and software development.

To get round this problem IBM invested $5 billion in developing System 360, a range of compatible machines all of which could run essentially the same software for either business or scientific applications. They varied in size from small, entry-level machines to powerful number crunchers. By standardising across the range, the company brought down the costs of its software and therefore made the hardware more attractive to customers. The industry standards established on System 360 remained essentially in place until the end of the mainframe era.

LEO III was in some respects more advanced than the most powerful of the System 360 models, particularly in its capacity for running three or four programs simultaneously. But, like most of IBM's other rivals, Scott now felt that he needed to develop his own range of compatible machines. He saw a new range as the only way to bring together the different 'clans' within English Electric Leo Marconi into a single team. At the same time, he knew he could not persuade the English Electric board to fund the development of the new products from scratch. Turning to the long-standing alliance between English Electric and RCA, he sent David Caminer to evaluate the American company's latest designs for a range known as Spectra 70. The Spectra 70 range was explicitly designed to be not only internally compatible, but also compatible with IBM machines. With some reservations, Caminer's team reported that Spectra 70 provided a good basis for a new range, and EELM pinned its future hopes on its own version of the RCA design which it called System 4.

EELM announced the new range with a great fanfare in September 1965, effectively curtailing any further attempt to market LEO III – despite the fact that even without a proper marketing campaign, its sales were increasing every year (from three in 1962 to eighteen in 1965). In the last months of 1964 Pinkerton's superb machine, and the team of consultants that championed it, had proved themselves by winning the biggest contract for commercial data processing ever offered in Europe, with the most demanding of customers in the UK, the General Post Office.

The GPO in the early 1960s had 400,000 employees, 6 million telephone subscribers, 15 million premium bond holders and 22 million accounts in the National Savings Bank. Its head of Organisation and Methods, Nick Smith, knew exactly what he wanted, and the Post Office engineers had all the skills needed to evaluate the technical quality of the machines on offer. The GPO had passed over the rather dated LEO II in 1956 when looking for a machine to run the postmen's payroll; but LEO III, and particularly the 326 model, was a different matter altogether. Nonetheless, David Caminer had to make the pitch of his life to win the contract in the face of competitors both from Britain and overseas who constantly cast doubts on the long-term future of the former Lyons subsidiary. He succeeded because the LEO 326 was the best machine for the job available at the time; and because Smith was confident that the Leo consultants would be able to work well with his own staff to bring the project to fruition.

The GPO bought two LEO IIIs in the first instance, and went on to buy five 326s to equip a series of National Data Processing Service centres, and to provide systems to manage the accounts in the National Savings Bank. The NDPS centres would issue Britain's telephone bills but would also carry out work for outside users. Anthony Wedgwood Benn MP (as he then was), then postmaster general in Harold Wilson's newly elected Labour government, personally announced the contract for the five LEO 326 models, worth around £2.5 million, in December 1964. 'It is very encouraging indeed,' Benn commented, 'to find that the British computer industry, after a long period in the doldrums, has at length shown it is consistently capable of standing up to, and beating on its merits, competition from over the seas.' By 1969, the Post Office had installed thirteen LEO IIIs and 326s at centres around the country.

There were other successes. Under David Caminer's indefatigable leadership, the sales team sold LEO IIIs in Australia and Czechoslovakia as well as South Africa. Shell Mex & BP, which had rejected LEO II in the 1950s in favour of a rival model, bought three of its more advanced siblings. The four Royal Dockyards bought one each, to run payrolls and monitor the distribution of labour for thousands of dock workers – the only time that Leo had won a sales contract from the Ministry of Defence. LEOs worked for Manchester Corporation and several London boroughs, a manufacturer of ladies' underwear, a mail order firm, the Inland Revenue, a bank, an insurance company and several other manufacturers. The eventual tally was fifty-nine LEO IIIs and 326s worldwide, nine overseas and the rest in the UK. This was a huge improvement on the eleven LEO IIs previously sold by Leo Computers Ltd. Additionally EELM sold twenty-seven KDF 9s for the scientific market in the same period.

Last Throw of the Dice

IBM's 1401, a general purpose computer system which had a transistorised processor, core store, magnetic tape drives and a fast printer, became available in 1960. It was not as advanced as the LEO III but it was cheaper and had the weight of a vast manufacturing, maintenance and sales organisation behind it. IBM eventually sold 12,000 of them: by 1964 there were 220 1401s in the United Kingdom alone. When it launched System 360 in 1964, even IBM's own factories were overwhelmed by the demand. Having taken a huge gamble, Thomas Watson Jr saw his $5 billion investment repaid within three years.

There was no company in Britain that could come anywhere near that performance. The biggest player was ICT, the company that had been formed from the merger of two office machines companies, British Tabulating Machines and Powers-Samas, in 1959. Since then it had acquired the computing interests of GEC and EMI, and in 1963 it absorbed its largest remaining British competitor, Ferranti. That left only four British companies – ICT, EELM, Elliott Automation and Plessey – struggling to survive in the sluggish British market against the might of IBM and other American companies such as Honeywell, UNIVAC and Control Data Systems.

As the British companies contemplated the overwhelming threat to their survival from across the Atlantic the British government, which had hitherto appeared wholly indifferent to the existence or otherwise of an indigenous computer industry, took an interest for the first time. In the year before his party's election, Harold Wilson caught the mood of the time when at the Labour Party conference he talked of 'the new Britain to be forged in the white heat of the technological revolution'. One of his first actions on coming to power was to establish a Ministry of Technology, with the trade unionist Frank Cousins as minister.

Murray Laver, who had spent much of his early career as a research engineer with the GPO, was appointed the chief scientist heading the new ministry's computer division. 'Mintech was set up as a pitchfork with four prongs to stick into the backside of Britain to get it moving,' he says. 'One of the prongs was computing.' The business historian David Jeremy notes that in 1964, when Mintech was set up, there were 22,000 computers in the United States, a quarter of which were in government departments. In the United Kingdom in the same year there were fewer than 1,000 computers in total, of which government departments owned only 56.

Mintech's first step in defence of the British computing industry was to introduce a protectionist purchasing policy within government: buy British if at all possible was the rule. 'If departments proposed to buy a non-British one – and quite a few of them did – we used to try and persuade them otherwise,' says Laver. 'If that didn't work at the level of officials, then Frank Cousins would talk to the minister; decisions even went to the Cabinet half a dozen times.'

It was a policy that certainly helped for a time. 'The net result was that we pretty well shared the market with ICT over the EEL period,' says John Aris, who was put in charge of government sales after Leo's merger with English Electric. The exception was the Ministry of Defence. 'MOD was big enough and ugly enough that if it wanted to do something contrary to government policy then it did it,' says Aris. 'We must have tendered for at least half a dozen contracts, and did not succeed at all apart from the Royal Dockyards.' MOD meanwhile bought IBM, UNIVAC and NCR machines, investing busily in American technology. This was a complete contrast to what was happening in the United States. The American Department of Defense had injected billions of dollars into its national computer industry, not only in sales but in funding for research and development. Kenneth Flamm, a senior fellow at the Brookings Institution in Washington DC, notes in his study of government, industry and high technology that 'for almost all US producers, the military was the first, and generally the best customer'.

Mintech was also unsuccessful in persuading some of the large, nationalised industries to work with common systems. The Post Office, always a pioneer, was already doing this at its regional National Data Processing Service centres. But others, such as the Gas Boards that served the different regions of the United Kingdom, each had their own accounting and billing systems. Mintech called a meeting to persuade their general managers of the savings in programming effort that could be made if they worked to a standard system. 'They all agreed that it was a splendid idea,' says Laver, 'and they would be perfectly ready to adopt a common system – as long as it was theirs. They weren't going to change. That was a great disillusionment to the junior minister, Jeremy Bray; he couldn't believe that people could be so irrational. Buying the computer and putting it in was the easiest part – what was so difficult was to change the way of thinking.' Laver and his colleagues did manage to set up a centre of excellence, the National Computing Centre in Manchester, to act as a common source of shared experience. Its first director, Gordon Black, was a mathematician from the Atomic Energy Authority, and in its early days the centre tended to be biased towards scientific rather than business computing. One of his successors, however, was John Aris, who learned his trade in the commercial environment of Leo Computers. The NCC remains in operation today, one of the few remaining legacies of the British government's belated attempt to play a strategic role in computer development.

Stimulating the market for business computers was a frustrating business for Laver. The gulf between the United States and the United Kingdom was almost as wide as it had been a decade before, when computers were first becoming available. 'The Americans would say "I hear old Joe's got a computer – we'd better have one in this company",' says Laver. 'The British would say "I hear old Joe's got a computer – let's see how he gets on with it." The only sign of progress I saw was that the managing directors of companies would say "I'm afraid I know nothing about computers", whereas five years before they would have said "I know nothing about computers, thank God."'

At the same time, computer manufacturers with a background in electrical engineering companies did not understand the extent to which their customers were going to need their help in defining their needs. The office machine companies at least knew their market, but tended to base their products on existing punched card systems rather than rethinking the job from scratch for a computer. 'There was really only one sophisticated user,' says Laver, 'and that was Lyons. And they made their own because they couldn't get anything suitable elsewhere.'

After two years, Anthony Wedgwood Benn replaced Frank Cousins as Minister of Technology. He felt that the British computer market, small as it was, could not support the number of suppliers that were competing for its attentions. There was no doubt that, with IBM spending more on R&D alone than the total turnover of all the British companies, none of them was in a position to compete effectively in the future. Benn and his officials, Laver among them, conceived the idea that Britain needed one big company rather than several small ones. 'We thought if we could accelerate the process of coalescence, this would build up something big enough to compete,' says Laver. Heading the negotiations was the ministry's tough permanent secretary, R. W. B. 'Otto' Clark. On the table was government funding for R&D – all of £20 million – in return for a merger that would absorb all the existing manufacturers.

'Mintech were in the Millbank Tower at that time,' says Laver, referring to a large office block near Westminster that later housed the headquarters of the Labour Party. 'The ministerial suite was on the 11th floor, which had a circular corridor with lifts at the opposite ends of the radius. The technique was to bring one party up in one lift while walking the other round to the opposite lift, so that they didn't meet. It was like a Whitehall farce.' The various parties were not keen on the idea of merging their separate identities – some specialising in communications and control, others in business computers – into some kind of amorphous conglomerate. But at a final, stormy meeting, Clark told the chairmen bluntly that if they wanted any government help at all, they had to go along with the merger, and on his – or rather the Treasury's – terms. They reluctantly agreed.

The first stage was English Electric Leo Marconi's absorption of the mainly military electronics firm Elliott Automation in 1967.

Rather than continuing the clumsy agglomeration of names it had adopted so far, the new company became simply English Electric Computers Ltd. The name of Leo was gone for good. The new company lasted only a year before it, in its turn, was merged with ICT and the computer division of another engineering firm, Plessey, to form International Computers Limited – ICL. ICL therefore became the only British manufacturer of computers (until the advent of microcomputer entrepreneurs such as Clive Sinclair with his ZX80, 81 and Spectrum and Alan Sugar with his Amstrad PC in the 1980s). The models of computer ICL began to produce, the 1900 and 2900, traced their descent from the series of scientific computers developed by Ferranti in association with engineers at Manchester University. In 1984 ICL was taken over by Standard Telephones and Cables (STC) – the same company that failed to produce a working magnetic tape drive for LEO I in the early 1950s. Since 1998 ICL has belonged to the Japanese information technology giant Fujitsu, and now operates under the name Fujitsu Services.

What went wrong? Not everyone agrees that the mergers forced on an unwilling industry in the late 1960s were, as Laver remembers, 'the only thing we could do'. Writing some years later in the journal *Computing*, Professor Stanley Gill, who had written the first primer for computer programmers with Maurice Wilkes and David Wheeler in 1951, argued that Benn had failed to rise to the challenge to 'undo the damage [the Whitehall establishment] had been doing to our computer industry since the latter began'. He added that, 'In comparison with what it could and should have been, the British computer industry is very little better today than it would have been if he had left it alone.' Maurice Wilkes agrees that 'the computer industry should have been left to sort itself out'.

Computer historians such as Martin Campbell-Kelly and John Hendry have analysed the reasons for the ultimate failure of the computing industry in a country that boasted innovators of the calibre of Alan Turing, Tommy Flowers, F. C. Williams, Tom Kilburn, Maurice Wilkes, David Wheeler – and Raymond Thompson, John Pinkerton, David Caminer and their colleagues at Lyons. The list is long: the reluctance of British management to see the advantages of computing; the small size of British computer companies relative to IBM and the other American companies; the apparent inability of British companies to combine effective salesmanship with technological innovation; the fact that by the end of the 1950s the British companies had allowed the Americans to open up a two-year gap in the application of new technologies such as transistors and magnetic tape.

But dwarfing all others in importance must be the role of government, particularly defence, investment. Campbell-Kelly reports that during the 1950s alone, IBM – an office machines company – won contracts worth almost $400 million from the US government, much of it for research and development. The British government, in contrast, appears never to have recognised the enormous commercial possibilities of business computing. The paltry sums available to the British computer industry through NRDC all went to electronics firms with defence interests – Ferranti, Elliott and EMI. NRDC invested £2 million, for example, in Ferranti's Atlas scientific computer, which on its appearance in 1963 briefly held the distinction of being the world's most powerful – but only four were ever built. Companies whose focus was on commercial data processing never saw a brass government farthing, other than through hard-won sales of hardware to government departments, until the period of mergers in the late 1960s – by which time it was all too late.

As for the individuals who were the industry's greatest resource, the wave of mergers fractured long-established loyalties and undermined the emotional ties to particular machines and ways of working. Few of the former Leo managers and senior consultants found themselves in positions of any influence within ICL.

Raymond Thompson had already gone. Unable to work with Wilf Scott at EEL, in 1966 he had accepted a post as computer adviser with Shell Mex & BP, having led the team that sold them three LEO IIIs. But the move was only a partial success. 'His best years were behind him,' says Land, 'and the people at Shell really didn't know who he was.' In 1976, shortly after his retirement, Thompson died during an operation for a heart problem that had been noticed by the Lyons company doctor twenty years before. Before going into hospital he had written a touching note to John Simmons, thanking him for his 'kindness, forbearance and help'.

Of the other Leo pioneers, Hemy had left long before to go to EMI; after it was taken over by ICT he moved to Unilever as a computer consultant. In his retirement he lived on the Scottish coast near Ayr and devoted himself to raising money for the local lifeboat service. He died in 2000. Ernest Lenaerts, an innovator to the last, worked on research projects related to the interactions between machines and their human operators, including speech recognition. But these projects were discontinued after the ICL merger, and Lenaerts took early retirement in 1969. He died in 1996. Leo Fantl was posted to South Africa in 1960 to set up and run a service bureau jointly between Leo Computers and Rand Mines, which was the first to introduce full-scale commercial computing to South Africa. After Rand took over the bureau he transferred to the company and settled in Johannesburg, later become managing director of Sage Computers there. He, too, died in 2000. Anthony Barnes, a former Leo board member and early programmer, left shortly after the merger with English Electric and apparently cut all ties with his former colleagues, none of whom can now say what he did subsequently. Frank Land, another pioneer programmer and later chief consultant, accepted an academic post at the London School of Economics at about the same time. In retirement he remains Visiting Professor of Information Management there.

Only John Pinkerton and David Caminer, of the original group at Lyons, survived through all the mergers to retirement. Pinkerton, the quietly spoken but brilliant engineer who had turned Simmons's dream into hardware reality, had the position of head of research after the merger with English Electric. He was designing an advanced new model to replace LEO III until Scott took the decision to base the new range on the Spectra 70. He never again enjoyed the intellectual and creative freedom he had been granted at Leo. He hid his disappointment by throwing his energies into helping the teenaged industry to establish uniform international standards, representing ICL on the European Computer Manufacturers' Association and twice serving as its president. Later, when the City of London extended its medieval apprenticeship system to computing by setting up the Worshipful Company of Information Technologists he became a founder member, devoting much time and energy to helping young people to enter the industry. After his retirement he worked as a consultant and pursued his long-term interests in music, photography, and debating all the issues of the day with his wife Helen. He was much mourned when he died in 1997, aged seventy-eight; since 2000 his memory has been kept alive by an annual lecture in his name sponsored by the Institution of Electrical Engineers.

David Caminer deplored the dispersal of Leo expertise effected by the more powerful ex-ICT managers after the merger: 'We should not have gone into ICL in such a subordinate position,' he says. As a senior executive within ICL he was given responsibility first for market planning, then for planning the system requirements of a new, unifying range of computers. As his final job before retiring he claimed a more hands-on role, heading a massive project to install a computer and communications system for the European Commission in Luxembourg with links to other European capitals, for which he was awarded the OBE. Since his retirement he has written extensively on the history of the LEO computers, and led the editing of a substantial collection of reminiscences by many of the key people involved (*User-Driven Innovation*, 1996).

LEO's Final Comeback

Just as an eclipse of the sun is preceded by a startling ring of brilliance, the story of Leo's decline had an uplifting coda. What was supposed to be the last LEO III had rolled out of the factory in 1967, and the engineers dispersed to other activities. But in 1969, soon after the formation of ICL, Murray Laver returned to the Post Office as Nick Smith's successor, and found that with telephone subscribers rising all the time, it needed extra capacity.

'My chaps came to me and said "We need to buy more LEOs and we don't know where to get them." So I had a meeting with the ICL people about making some more, and they said, "You can't be serious!" And I said, "I am serious."' ICL wanted the Post Office to wait until the new range, then in development, was ready – but that would not be for three years. Laver said he could not wait. Eventually ICL agreed to make five more LEO 326s – as long as the Post Office did not embarrass them by publicising the fact.

'We were very fond of LEOs,' says Laver. 'They just worked – there was no reason to change them.' Several of the Post Office LEOs eventually enjoyed working lives of up to fifteen years. The last few came out of service in 1981 – thirty years after LEO I had run the world's first office job.

Epilogue

It was always a Lyons tradition to mark important moments with some ceremony. On 4 January 1965 the company invited journalists, LEO's creators and other guests to witness a poignant farewell. At 6 p.m. the operator turned off LEO I, still working faithfully for Lyons after fourteen years, for the last time. Raymond Thompson paid a few words of tribute to a machine that had 'seeded a great industry', and press reports in the days that followed documented the already archaic machine's list of first achievements. And then LEO I was broken up, a few parts going as mementoes to the Science Museum, the valuable mercury in the delay lines sold for scrap.

The first of the LEOs to be sold commercially – indeed, the first computer sold for commercial use in the United Kingdom – received a similarly emotional send-off in 1971. LEO II/3, installed at Stewarts & Lloyds steelworks in 1958, had been used continuously since then. 'I don't suppose we shall ever again keep a computer in service as long as this one,' said Neil Pollock, the manager of Organisation and Methods at Stewarts & Lloyds.

The longevity of the early LEOs hinged not so much on the design of their hardware, which was outdated for much of their lives, but on the systems David Caminer and his team of consultants developed to run on them. The whole LEO philosophy depended on working in partnership with a company with a similarly progressive outlook to develop a system tailored to the company's needs. But that philosophy in the end contributed to the demise of the LEO

On 4 January 1965 old LEO hands gathered to witness the last moments of LEO I. (Front row, from left) John Pinkerton, Raymond Thompson, John Simmons, Anthony Salmon. David Caminer is at the extreme right.

brand. Few companies were prepared to rethink their whole approach to management before they installed a computer, and the market quickly began to favour off-the-peg systems that could supposedly be made to do whatever you wanted.

Since I began to write this book, there have been several front-page stories about computer installations. In every case what makes the story is the fact that it has been a spectacular and expensive failure for a well-known institution. The Passport Office,

Cambridge University, the Ministry of Defence, the Child Support Agency: in every case a system bought at huge expense has turned out not to be usable by the people who need it. One of the recurring themes of a conference held to celebrate '50 Years of Business Computing' in December 2001 – dating from the first running of Bakery Valuations on LEO I – was the unsolved problem of ensuring that new systems would succeed.

The LEO experiment, quixotic as it may have been in the context of a large catering company, is worth remembering for much more than being the first. It is worth remembering because its architects never forgot what the computer was for: it was a tool for business, and so it was their responsibility to make sure it worked for business. Maybe that is the lesson that the designers of modern systems would do well to remember.

Leo people retain a sense of attachment to a piece of British history that they keep alive through regular reunions and a well-tended website (www.leo-computers.org.uk). These activities exude an atmosphere of camaraderie and shared pride: 'They say you always remember your first love,' wrote one correspondent to the website, 'and in terms of things mechanical – and the LEO was certainly that – I can safely say that no other computer I've worked on in a long career have I held in as much affection as the LEO.'

Devotion to LEO has remained a rather specialised passion – the computers never reached a wide enough audience to share the place in the national affections enjoyed by its owners' better-known creations, the Lyons teashops. But every now and then the story is retold, through books, TV, radio and newspaper articles, and a new generation can wonder at the extraordinary achievements of a small group of people who invented the business computer in a valiant attempt to keep the teashops in business.

Sources

LEO and Lyons

Aris, Stephen, *The Jews in Business*, Cape, 1970.

Beable, William H., *Romance of Great Businesses*, Heath Cranton, 1926.

Bird, Peter, *LEO: The First Business Computer*, Hasler Publishing, 1994.

—, *The First Food Empire*, Phillimore, 2000.

Bridges, Thomas C. and H. Hessell Tiltman, *Kings of Commerce*, Harrap, 1928.

Caminer, David, John Aris, Peter Hermon and Frank Land (eds), *User-Driven Innovation* (published in the United States as *LEO: The Incredible Story of the World's First Business Computer*), McGraw-Hill, 1996, 1998.

Evans, Chris, interview with John Pinkerton, *Annals of the History of Computing*, vol. 5, (1975), pp. 64–72.

Hendry, John, 'The Teashop Computer Manufacturer: J. Lyons and the Potential and Limits of High-Tech Diversification', *Business History*, vol. 29, (1987), pp. 73–102.

Jeremy, David J., *A Business History of Britain 1900–1990s*, Oxford University Press, 1998.

LEO Archive (NAHC/LEO), National Archive of the History of Computing, John Rylands University Library of Manchester.

Lyons Archive (ACC/3527), London Metropolitan Archive.

Salmon, Julian, 'Development and Organisation of J. Lyons &

Company Ltd.', in *Business Growth*, ed. by Ronald S. Edwards and Harry Townsend, Macmillan, 1966, pp. 163–77.

Simmons, John, *LEO and the Managers*, Macdonald, 1962.

—, Papers (MSS.363), Modern Records Centre, University of Warwick.

Computer History

Aspray, William, *John von Neumann and the Origins of Modern Computing*, MIT Press, 1990.

Bashe, Charles J. et al., *IBM's Early Computers*, MIT Press, 1986.

Berkeley, Edmund C., *Giant Brains, or Machines that Think*, Wiley, 1949.

Campbell-Kelly, Martin, *ICL: A Business and Technical History*, Oxford University Press, 1989.

Campbell-Kelly, Martin, and William Aspray, *Computer: A History of the Information Machine*, Basic Books, 1996.

Ceruzzi, Paul E., *A History of Modern Computing*, MIT Press, 1998.

Cortada, James W., *Before the Computer: IBM, Burroughs and Remington Rand and the Industry they Created*, Princeton University Press, 1993.

Darwin, Charles, 'Douglas Rayner Hartree 1897–1958', *Biographical Memoirs of the Fellows of the Royal Society*, vol. 4 (1958), pp. 103–16.

Flamm, Kenneth, *Creating the Computer: Government, Industry and High Technology*, The Brookings Institution, 1988.

Goldstine, Herman, *The Computer from Pascal to von Neumann*, Princeton University Press, 1972.

Halsbury, Rt Hon. the Earl of, 'Ten Years of Computer Development', *Computer Journal*, vol. 1, no. 1 (1959), pp. 153–9.

Hartree, Douglas, *Calculating Machines: Recent and Prospective Developments*, Cambridge University Press, 1947.

Hendry, John, *Innovating for Failure: Government Policy and the Early British Computer Industry*, MIT Press, 1990.

Hodges, Andrew, *Alan Turing: The Enigma*, Vintage, 1992.

Lavington, Simon, *Early British Computers*, Manchester University Press, 1980.

Menabrea, Luigi, 'Sketch of the Analytical Engine Invented by Charles Babbage Esq.' (with Notes by Ada Lovelace), *Taylor's Scientific Memoirs*, vol. 3 (1843), article XIX.

Singh, Simon, *The Code Book*, Fourth Estate, 1999.

Swade, Doron, *The Cogwheel Brain*, Little, Brown, 2000.

Turing, A. M., 'On Computable Numbers, with an Application to the *Entscheidungsproblem*', *Proceedings of the London Mathematical Society*, Series 2, vol. 42 (1936–7), pp. 230–65.

Wilkes, Maurice, *Memoirs of a Computer Pioneer*, MIT, 1985.

Wilkes, Maurice, David Wheeler and Stanley Gill, *The Preparation of Programs for an Electronic Digital Computer*, Addison-Wesley, 1951, reprinted by Tomash Publishers, 1982.

Winterbotham, F. W., *The Ultra Secret*, Weidenfeld and Nicolson, 1974.

Scientific Management, Office Work and Automation

Babbage, Charles, *On the Economy of Machinery and Manufactures*, 4th edn., C. Knight, 1835, reissued Routledge/Thoemmes, 1993.

Bowden, B. V., *Faster than Thought*, Pitman, 1953.

Campbell, William, *Office Practice*, Pitman, 1933.

Delgado, Alan, *The Enormous File: A Social History of the Office*, John Murray, 1979.

Diebold, John, *Automation: The Advent of the Automatic Factory*, Van Nostrand, 1952.

—, *Beyond Automation: Managerial Problems of an Exploding Technology*, McGraw-Hill, 1964.

Kanigel, Robert, *The One Best Way: Frederick Winslow Taylor and the Enigma of Efficiency*, Little, Brown, 1997.

Leffingwell, W. H., *Scientific Office Management*, Shaw, 1917.

—, *Office Management: Principles and Practice*, Shaw, 1926.

—, *A Textbook of Office Management*, McGraw-Hill, 1932; 3rd edn. (with E. M. Robinson), 1950.

Lockwood, David, *The Blackcoated Worker: A Study in Class Consciousness*, Oxford University Press, 2nd edn., 1989.

Macmillan, Robert, *Automation: Friend or Foe?*, Cambridge University Press, 1956.

Mills, Geoffrey, and Oliver Standingford, *Office Organization and Method*, Pitman, 1949.

Mumford, Edith, and Olive Banks, *The Computer and the Clerk*, Routledge and Kegan Paul, 1967.

Office Management Association, *Electronics in the Office*, 1957.

Rhee, H. A., *Office Automation in Social Perspective*, Basil Blackwell, 1968.

Standingford, Oliver, *Office: A book about Administrative Management*, BBC, 1972.

Taylor, F. W., *The Principles of Scientific Management*, Harper, 1923.

Urwick, L., and E. F. L. Brech, *The Making of Scientific Management*, Management Publications Trust, 1945.

Williams, R. H., *The Electronic Office*, Gee, 2nd edn., 1958.

Picture Credits

Index

Figures in italics indicate captions.